www.wadsworth.com

wadsworth.com is the World Wide Web site for
Wadsworth Publishing Company and is your direct
source to dozens of online resources.

At *wadsworth.com* you can find out about supplements,
demonstration software, and student resources. You can
also send e-mail to many of our authors and preview new
publications and exciting new technologies.

wadsworth.com
Changing the way the world learns®

Challenging Your Preconceptions

Thinking Critically about Psychology

SECOND EDITION

Randolph A. Smith

Ouachita Baptist University

WADSWORTH

THOMSON LEARNING

Australia • Canada • Mexico • Singapore • Spain
United Kingdom • United States

WADSWORTH

THOMSON LEARNING

Psychology Publisher: *Edith Beard Brady*
Assistant Editor: *Julie Dillemuth*
Editorial Assistant: *Maritess A. Tse*
Marketing Manager: *Joanne Terhaar*
Marketing Assistant: *Justine Ferguson*
Project Manager, Editorial Production:
Erica Silverstein
Print/Media Buyer: *Robert King*
Permissions Editor: *Robert Kauser*

Text Designer: *Anne Draus, Scratchgravel*
Publishing Services
Copy Editor: *Cathy Baebler*
Cover Designer and Illustrator:
Carole Lawson
Text and Cover Printer: *Webcom Limited*
Compositor: *Scratchgravel Publishing*
Services

Printed in Canada
1   2   3   4   5   6   7   05   04   03   02   01

Wadsworth/Thomson Learning
10 Davis Drive
Belmont, CA 94002-3098
USA

For more information about our products,
contact us:
Thomson Learning Academic Resource
Center
1-800-423-0563
http://www.wadsworth.com

International Headquarters
Thomson Learning
International Division
290 Harbor Drive, 2nd Floor
Stamford, CT 06902-7477
USA

UK/Europe/Middle East/South Africa
Thomson Learning
Berkshire House
168-173 High Holborn
London WC1V 7AA
United Kingdom

Asia
Thomson Learning
60 Albert Street, #15-01
Albert Complex
Singapore 189969

Canada
Nelson Thomson Learning
1120 Birchmount Road
Toronto, Ontario M1K 5G4
Canada

Library of Congress Cataloging-in-Publication Data

Smith, Randolph A.
    Challenging your preconceptions : thinking critically about psychology / Randolph A. Smith.—2nd ed.
        p.   cm.
    Includes bibliographical references and index.
    ISBN 0-534-26739-4
    1. Psychology.   2. Critical thinking.   I. Title.
BF121 .S577 2001
150—dc20   2001026298

To Corliss—
for your support, inspiration, and encouragement

Contents

Preface

Psychology is about critical thinking; life is about critical thinking. Many instructors try to teach critical thinking in their classrooms and hope that it will transfer to the real world. I have tried to create a book that will help them in this task. Its focus is critical thinking in controversial, confusing, and interesting psychological issues. Thus, it teaches critical thinking not in a vacuum but in context. As the book's title implies, I approach this task by challenging students to avoid their preconceptions, which often impede critical thinking.

Although the book is designed primarily as a supplement to an introductory psychology course, it could also be used as a stand-alone text or as a supplement in other courses. Chapter 1 introduces the guidelines for critical thinking that form the framework of the book. Each chapter after Chapter 1 fits with one of the chapters of most traditional introductory texts. In these chapters, students are reacquainted with the critical thinking guidelines through an examination of the critical thinking errors that occur when someone falls prey to his or her preconceived notions. "Thinking about Preconceptions" sections alert students to ways they can think critically about the concepts covered. Finally, "Critical Thinking Challenges" are provided in each chapter so students can test their skills in hypothetical situations.

Topics covered in each chapter include the following:

Chapter 1 (Guidelines for Critical Thinking): Introduction
Chapter 2 (Psychology and the Popular Press): How to critically read about psychology
Chapter 3 (Statistical Seduction): Statistics and research

lll

Chapter 4 (Anatomy Is Destiny—Or Is It?): Biological bases
of behavior

Chapter 5 (Is What You See What You Get?): Sensation and
perception

Chapter 6 (Can Hypnosis Help Me Remember?): Altered
states of consciousness

Chapter 7 (Conditioning and Advertising): Learning

Chapter 8 (Biases in Memory): Memory

Chapter 9 (IQ Is Forever—Isn't It?): Testing

Chapter 10 (Understanding Our Own Motives): Motivation

Chapter 11 (Evaluating Codependency): Abnormal behavior

Chapter 12 (Is Bibliotherapy Helpful?): Therapy

Chapter 13 (Social Influence Tactics): Social psychology

I've enjoyed digging through various research topics to
create this book. I hope you find it helpful.

Acknowledgments

There are many people I would like to thank for their help and
contributions to the evolution of this book. First and foremost
among these is Wayne Weiten, who helped conceive the idea for
this book, encouraged me to write it, and provided me with
ideas and feedback along the way.

The Wadsworth staff has been a delight to work with. I
value the advice and feedback I've received from Publisher Edith
Beard Brady and Associate Project Manager Erica Silverstein on
this second edition (and Claire Verduin on the first edition).
Maritess Tse (Editorial Asssistant), Joanne Terhaar (Marketing
Manager), Bob Kauser (Permissions Manager), and Lisa Weber
(Project Manager) have also provided valuable help in their areas
of expertise.

On my campus, I owe a great debt of gratitude to Janice
Ford of the Ouachita Baptist University Library, who obtained
many reference materials for me through interlibrary loans.

This book has benefitted from helpful reviewers in both
editions. I appreciate the input from Steven Berman (Florida International University), Bryan Fantie (American University), Brad
Redburn (Johnson County Community College), and Chris
Wetzel (Rhodes College) in helping to shape this revision. I re-

main indebted to Drew Appleby (IUPUI), Barney Beins (Ithaca College), James Calhoun (University of Georgia), and Jack Kirschenbaum (Fullerton College) for their reviews of the first edition of the book.

In addition to Wayne Weiten, who contributed ideas and input for the book in general, three other individuals provided in-depth help on particular chapters. I thank Chris Spatz for his wisdom in Chapter 3, Catherine Fichten for information that helped me write Chapter 2, and Gerald Rosen for the information and input he provided for Chapter 12.

Finally, I am indebted to a variety of people for their help in developing my critical thinking skills. My psychology professors at the University of Houston and Texas Tech University got me started in the right direction. Many APA Division Two colleagues have been inspirational and informational over the years. Randall Wight, a colleague at Ouachita, has challenged me to think at new levels. And, finally, thanks to my critical thinking role models, Jane Halonen and Diane Halpern—you've been marvelous.

To the Student

Why should you read a book about critical thinking and psychology? Surely, you think, most psychology textbooks already contain more than enough information; why add even more reading to your psychology course? Among the many possible reasons, I consider three to be particularly valid.

First, you must be able to think critically in order to be well educated. Critics of the American education system maintain that we are falling behind other countries in educating students, particularly in the area of thinking. For example, the National Commission on Excellence in Education (1983), in assessing the state of education in America, noted that "many 17-year-olds do not possess the 'higher order' intellectual skills we should expect of them. Nearly 40% cannot draw inferences from written material . . ." (p. 9). Several major reports issued in the 1980s maintained that America must stress the development of critical thinking skills to stay competitive with the rest of the world (Brookfield, 1987). America's report cards for the 1990s were no better. How does this need for critical thinking impact you personally? Critical thinking skills ensure your competitiveness and competence in the world of work. No matter what career you plan to pursue, change is likely to be the most important word used to describe careers in the future. Students entering college today are told that the average worker will change careers several times. In fact, it is probable that many of today's students will eventually have careers in fields that do not even exist yet. In situations involving such a high degree of change, the ability to think well is going to be much more useful than any specific skill or information you learned in college.

Second, it is important for you to be able to think critically in this age of the "information explosion." Today we are creating more new information at a faster rate than ever before. According to Wurman (1989), the amount of information available to us doubles about every five years. Not all of this new information is correct, beneficial, or useful. Therefore, you have to be able to separate the "wheat from the chaff"—and do it quickly. The guidelines for critical thinking presented in Chapter 1 will help you in this task. I hope you will learn from observing what critical thinkers do and model some of their behaviors in your thinking. If so, you will be on your way to gaining the type of education that will serve you well both now and in the future.

Third, modern life confronts us with a relentless parade of psychological issues, so the ability to think critically about psychological questions and ideas is crucial. As we go through life, many of the practical problems that we encounter—such as coping with stress, improving relationships, or discerning people's motives—are actually psychological issues because they concern questions about behavior. To solve these problems effectively, you must use critical thinking skills. In this book, we will examine many controversial topics and intriguing sets of findings, all within the field of psychology. In each chapter, you will encounter information about a specific topic and will use the guidelines from Chapter 1 to evaluate the details critically. This will entail work on your part—no one ever said that thinking critically is easy—but you will find the work challenging and informative. For example, finding the hidden preconceptions behind an argument can be as exciting as a lawyer's finding holes in a witness's testimony. Each chapter ends with questions and assignments that can help you learn to think critically without having someone guide you through the necessary steps.

Let's proceed to Chapter 1 and find out what critical thinkers do that makes them efficient thinkers and problem solvers. By using them as models, you can substantially improve your critical thinking skills.

Randolph A. Smith

References for Preface

Brookfield, S. D. (1987). *Developing critical thinkers*. San Francisco: Jossey-Bass.

National Commission on Excellence in Education. (1983). *A nation at risk: The imperative for educational reform*. Washington, DC: U.S. Department of Education.

Wurman, R. S. (1989). *Information anxiety*. New York: Doubleday.

Challenging Your Preconceptions

1

❦

Guidelines for Critical Thinking

You might wonder why this book begins with a chapter about how critical thinkers think. Do people really think in different ways? Don't we all think alike? Psychologists have asked similar questions for many years.

Some psychologists have believed that we all think in a similar manner. Jean Piaget, a famous developmental psychologist, conceived of critical thinking as a natural product of cognitive development in which children's thinking processes mature and become more adultlike. According to Piaget, children usually begin moving from the concrete operations stage of cognitive development to the formal operations stage around age 11 (Renner, 1976). This transition enables the child to go beyond thinking that requires manipulating concrete objects. The formal operations stage of thought allows the child to contemplate the possibility of new and different worlds beyond what he or she has experienced, to hypothesize about relationships between objects and events, and to contemplate thinking itself. Formal operational thought, according to Piaget, is the most advanced mode of thought and is crucial for critical thinking.

Piaget believed that most people complete the formal operations stage by about age 16 and are then capable of abstract thought and critical thinking. However, research has indicated that this assumption may be overly optimistic. The National Commission on Excellence in Education (1983) found that many 17-year-olds lacked higher thinking skills. McKinnon (1976) tested 185 freshmen at seven different colleges and found only 42.7% of them operating at the formal operational level. Meyers (1986) wrote that many middle-aged adults still function at the concrete operations level in at least some areas.

These data imply that many people think at a level that makes effective critical thinking difficult.

Thus, it appears that Piaget was wrong—we don't all think alike. It seems that some people develop the capacity for more advanced thought that enables them to think critically whereas others do not. What makes highly skilled critical thinkers different? You'll find out in this chapter.

Research shows that experts can solve problems that novices cannot handle because experts have an edge in knowledge and have had more experience in their area of expertise (Halpern, 1996). I hope that this book will help you become more expert in critical thinking by giving you both knowledge about and practice in thinking critically. Combined with your psychology text, this book will give you a knowledge base in psychology that is necessary to think critically about the discipline.

To this point, I have not yet defined critical thinking for you. There is no consensus definition, so you can find different ideas when you look at different sources. For our purposes, I will define critical thinking as *a logical and rational process of avoiding one's preconceptions by gathering evidence, contemplating and evaluating alternatives, and coming to a conclusion*. To expand on this definition, let's examine some guidelines for critical thinking.

Critical Thinking Guidelines

In devising this list, I consulted many experts in the critical thinking field, looking at their descriptions of critical thinkers. I developed a consensual list—one that is composed of characteristics that several writers mentioned, even if their terminologies differ somewhat (Bransford & Stein, 1993; Brookfield, 1987; Halonen, 1986; Halpern, 1996; Mayer & Goodchild, 1990; Wade & Tavris, 1990).

1. Critical thinkers are flexible—they can tolerate ambiguity and uncertainty. In short, critical thinkers are open-minded. Being a critical thinker often requires avoiding neat compartmentalizations of the world, refraining from black-and-white analyses of complex questions. If you enjoy mysteries and complexities and are willing to wonder, you have some important qualities of critical thinkers. Fictional detectives such as Sherlock Holmes and those in movies and TV shows are often able to solve cases because they deal well with uncertainty. Rather than jumping to a seemingly obvious conclusion, they remain open-minded and continue looking at additional clues and suspects. Critical thinkers are willing to question and test their ideas and assumptions. Many of us have such a strong desire to settle matters that we would close a case (and our minds) at the first available opportunity. When you hear complex questions in psychology cast in "either-or" terms (for example, heredity OR environment used to explain behavior), be sure to remember this point.

   2. Critical thinkers identify inherent biases and assumptions. We are often faced with statements and claims that are heavily loaded with biases and assumptions. (Advertising claims are prime examples.) You may remember statements people made as you grew up—for example, "All people on welfare are lazy and are cheating the government. They could get jobs if they wanted to." As you grew older and looked more critically at the world around you, you may have questioned such statements. Perhaps you realized those people making those statements worked hard at their jobs and resented their increasing tax burden. They may have known people who defrauded the government through the welfare system. This information gave you the background necessary to understand generalizations about people who receive welfare. Thus, you learned that people's beliefs and experiences play a role in their biases and assumptions. Most, if not all, statements (even yours) have biases and assumptions behind them. Biases and assumptions do not necessarily make statements wrong, but we should be alert to that possibility. Psychologists (and other scientists) who develop theories may well have blind spots about what research data have to say about their favorite theory.

   3. Critical thinkers maintain an air of skepticism. When you were a young child, you probably believed most things people told you. Remember how you heard that eating vegetables would make you grow up big and strong? As you grew older, you became a more critical consumer of information. When you again heard that comment about vegetables, you may have responded with "Really?" or "Oh yeah?" So you began your questioning approach to the world. As you grew still older, you became more sophisticated and wanted some evidence about the health benefits of vegetables, perhaps demanding "Prove it!" We often develop this skeptical approach as we age, although we don't always use it.

Many times we question information or ideas only when they do not fit with our preconceived notions. To be critical thinkers, we need to maintain a skeptical attitude even about ideas with which we agree. We need to train ourselves to question statements and claims—not only those made by politicians, medical quacks, and talk-show hosts, but also those by people we like and respect. Psychologists and teachers should not be exempt from this notion—you will learn much more about psychology if you question the ideas and theories you read in your text and hear about in class. If you have been around a 4- or 5-year-old recently, you know that young children learn a great deal about the world by asking questions. The same holds true for adults, as long as we question critically. Often the only way to learn that we have made an error is to be questioned about the matter. Thus, an important part of science is the willingness to self-correct—to look for errors and work to correct them.

4. *Critical thinkers separate facts from opinions.* A major difference between scientists and nonscientists is the requirement of evidence when making a decision. You may remember trying to convince your parents to allow you to stay out later than normal with the opinionated argument "It's OK for me to stay out late—everyone else does." When your parents questioned you further, you admitted that "everyone else" was your best friend and some other teenager you had heard about. Your desire to stay out later led you to confuse opinion with fact. When we draw conclusions about empirical matters, we need to rely on scientific evidence. Scientists strive to be objective. In relying on objective evidence, psychologists use scientific methods of data gathering such as laboratory and field research.

Many students who take a psychology course prefer to rely on personal experiences rather than on scientific evidence. Thus, students often have difficulty dealing with a general finding of psychology when it contradicts their personal experience. However, we should remember that isolated cases may not be consistent with general findings. It is generally better to rely on facts derived from a variety of settings and individuals than to base conclusions on opinions we hold or that we get from others. In order to rely on facts rather than opinions, we must remain emotionally detached when dealing with thorny issues. Emotional involvement often leads us to argue from an opinionated position. Pay special attention to the early sections of your introductory psychology text that discuss research methodology and statistics—this information will give you some helpful hints for separating facts and opinions.

5. Critical thinkers don't oversimplify. Although simple explanations of behavior are appealing, they are often too simplistic to be correct. The world is a complicated place in which complex causation is the rule rather than the exception. Because of this complexity, we must look beyond easy and obvious alternatives when answering questions. Avoiding oversimplification requires us to think divergently—to imagine and explore alternative explanations. Thinking in a divergent manner is sometimes difficult. Much of our education has trained us to think convergently—to hone in on one correct answer. When thinking critically, we must realize that there may be more than one correct way of answering a question. For example, you may have applied to a college that rejected you solely on the basis of your SAT or ACT score. This experience was frustrating because you believed that your college grades would reflect more than what one standardized test score could show. College boards that rely only on test scores to determine admission are guilty of oversimplified thinking. Although using test scores alone makes such decisions easy, these colleges may be missing many qualified students who do not fare well on standardized tests, who had a bad day when they were tested, or who tested low for any number of reasons. This is why many colleges use a variety of criteria in making admission decisions. Similarly, many (all?) psychological traits and behaviors are much too complex to be explained by a single variable. Watch out for oversimplified explanations throughout your course!

6. Critical thinkers use logical inference processes. We draw inferences when we make hypotheses indirectly based on information that is given to us. Bransford and Stein (1993) and Halpern (1996) noted that we make inferences extensively to understand people when they talk to us. When Sally tells you that she is going to bed at 9:00 P.M. even though her usual bedtime is midnight, you draw some inference—she may be overly tired, she may not feel good, or she may have to get up early in the morning. These are logical inferences because they follow reasonably from the information given. It would not be logical to infer that Sally is tired because she has been zapped by an alien space ray that is sapping her strength. This inference is possible, but certainly not probable.

Critical thinkers use logical inference processes and check to see whether other people also make logical inferences. Inconsistencies in statements and conclusions often signal that illogical inferences have been made. If an assertion is based on illogical reasoning, the assertion isn't likely to be accurate or valid. During your psychology class, if a conclusion does not seem to follow logically from the evidence presented, don't simply read on. Stop, reread the information, and think about it. If necessary, ask your teacher to help you with the logic involved. You will get better at making logical inferences through practice.

7. *Critical thinkers examine available evidence before drawing conclusions.* Effective critical thinkers appreciate the need to consult diverse sources of information. If we examine only one source of information, we may fall prey to a particular set of biased assumptions. It is usually easier to discover the biases underlying a specific position by looking at a variety of positions. Once we have examined several sources, we can then think in a convergent manner. As we sift the available evidence, we hope to find the bulk of the evidence favoring one possible conclusion so we can decide in favor of it. Your textbook author will have done much of this work for you—for example, you will probably read about several theories of personality or abnormal behavior.

However, you should remember that one idea or position may not stand out from all the others. Authors are often not able to tell you which theory is "correct." Critical thinking does not guarantee that we will be able to eliminate all the alternatives except one. If critical thinking allows us to eliminate one or more of the alternatives, we have made important progress.

Conclusion

Even after reaching a conclusion through critical thinking, good critical thinkers realize that they must continue to use these seven guidelines so that new preconceptions do not blind them to alternative ideas. The reason for maintaining an open mind even after making a decision is relatively simple but very important: "Facts" can change over time. This point is probably at odds with what you have thought about facts for most of your life. However, "facts" simply represent our state of knowledge at any given point in time. Think about various "facts" that have been disproved throughout history: The sun revolves around the Earth, leeches must be used to bleed people to help them recover from various diseases, people cannot fly, and space travel is impossible. It is easy to look back at these earlier beliefs and be amused at how gullible people were. Yet in 50 or 100 years people may draw the same conclusion about us. "Facts" in psychology have also changed over the years, as you will discover in your study of the discipline. Thus, it is conceivable that "facts" you learn in your current psychology course will be discarded in 25, 10, or even 5 years.

The notion that facts can become outdated emphasizes the importance of critical thinking. Critical thinking does not teach you a set of facts. Instead, it gives you a way of thinking about facts and testing those facts to determine whether they are adequate. Thus, critical thinking about any topic goes on and on. Even when we believe that we have arrived at a correct answer or explanation, we should continue to question it as we gather new information. Critical thinking involves a lifetime of learning—a dynamic, ongoing process that does not stop. I challenge you to adopt a critical thinking approach not only to your psychology class and to psychological information, but throughout your entire life. Medical claims, your world of work, and political choices, just to name a few, are challenges that cry out for critical analysis.

We all typically have preconceptions about issues we face; critical thinking is necessary to test these preconceptions. When we merely restate our preconceived ideas, we are not thinking critically. Our assumptions and preconceptions help to determine how we see the world, limit the choices we make, and dictate the behaviors we choose. Thus, to become critical thinkers, we must confront our biases.

Our biases often make us close-minded about a certain issue or topic. Although we realize that there are two sides to every story, we often think of those two sides as "my side" and "the wrong side." To be critical thinkers, we must familiarize ourselves with all sides of an issue and remain flexible and open-minded. Many people do not think critically because they do not want to deal with ambiguity and uncertainty. Relying on assumptions and preconceptions insulates them from having to deal with such vagueness. Thinking critically requires that we accept the uncertainties and continue to question and test ideas and assumptions.

Even when we resolve to find out all we can about the various viewpoints concerning an issue, we must be careful in making judgments about the accuracy of these viewpoints. The view that we like the most or that seems to make the most sense to us is not necessarily the correct one. Our assumptions and preconceptions are often based on such reasoning, but we must learn to rely on scientific evidence to draw conclusions about psychological issues.

In this chapter, we defined seven guidelines for critical thinkers. We need to use these guidelines so that our preconceptions won't block our critical thinking. Now it is time for you to apply the guidelines and characteristics to actual psychological concepts and controversies. *Happy thinking!*

References

Bransford, J. D., & Stein, B. S. (1993). *The ideal problem solver* (2nd ed.). New York: W. H. Freeman.

Brookfield, S. D. (1987). *Developing critical thinkers*. San Francisco: Jossey-Bass.

Halonen, J. S. (Ed.). (1986). *Teaching critical thinking in psychology*. Milwaukee, WI: Alverno College.

Halpern, D. F. (1996). *Thought and knowledge: An introduction to critical thinking* (3rd ed.). Mahwah, NJ: Erlbaum.

Mayer, R., & Goodchild, F. (1990). *The critical thinker*. Dubuque, IA: William C. Brown.

McKinnon, J. W. (1976). The college student and formal operations. In J. W. Renner, D. G. Stafford, A. E. Lawson, J. W. McKinnon, F. E. Friot, & D. H. Kellogg (Eds.), *Research, teaching, and learning with the Piaget model* (pp. 110–129). Norman: University of Oklahoma Press.

Meyers, C. (1986). *Teaching students to think critically*. San Francisco: Jossey-Bass.

National Commission on Excellence in Education. (1983). *A nation at risk: The imperative for educational reform*. Washington, DC: U.S. Department of Education.

Renner, J. W. (1976). Formal operational thought and its identification. In J. W. Renner, D. G. Stafford, A. E. Lawson, J. W. McKinnon, F. E. Friot, & D. H. Kellogg (Eds.), *Research, teaching, and learning with the Piaget model* (pp. 64–78). Norman: University of Oklahoma Press.

Wade, C., & Tavris, C. (1990). *Learning to think critically: The case of close relationships* (2nd ed.). New York: HarperCollins.

2

🌿

Psychology and the Popular Press

Many students who enroll in psychology courses are convinced that they already know something about psychology because they have read about psychology in the popular press—the newspapers and magazines found in supermarkets and bookstores. In almost any newspaper or popular magazine there is at least one article that relates to psychology in some way. These articles are typically not written by psychologists. Rather, psychologists publish their research articles in psychology journals. It is the job of popular press writers to distill complex information from these journals so that we readers can learn about a variety of topics that we don't have the time, energy, or expertise to research on our own. Thus, the popular press serves what I call a *Reader's Digest* function for us—it condenses large amounts of information into an easy-to-read, easy-to-understand format. This condensation is an important and valuable function in light of the information explosion we are experiencing today.

You have probably concluded by now that there must be a shortcoming of some sort in the manner that the popular press handles psychology. If the popular press performed perfectly on this count, then why would this topic appear in this book? If you have already jumped to this conclusion, you made a logical inference—good thinking on your part!

Guidelines for Reading Articles from the Popular Press

Rubenstein (1976) advocated that we should develop skills for reading about professional information in the popular press. First, we should recognize the difference between a summary of a report and a complete report. The popular press exists primarily to alert us to important information and provides only a summary of findings, omitting many details. The lack of details usually makes it difficult for us to critically evaluate evidence about a topic.

Second, we should be familiar with different types of evidence and the types of conclusions we can draw from each. Personal experience and anecdotal evidence are not usually considered good scientific evidence. Although these approaches may be used as a source of ideas or hypotheses, they do not provide verifying or validating information. A good critical thinker is able to distinguish empirical evidence from opinion-based ideas. Critical thinkers do not draw conclusions from evidence that will not support those conclusions. The popular press often does not provide enough information to enable us to critically evaluate the evidence.

Third, we need to beware of stretching the results of a single study too far. The popular press, in an attempt to dramatize a particular finding, may present the reported research as a major discovery or breakthrough. Rubenstein pointed out that such dramatic findings are rare. The scientific process is a slow one; it makes progress in small steps that are repeatedly verified before being fully accepted. Thus, critical thinkers view a single report linking marijuana use and chromosomal damage or a study that finds hormonal factors in homosexuality with a healthy degree of skepticism. Subsequent research may point to flaws in the original finding.

Fourth, we should remember that the popular press is designed to be popular. That is, writers are selective about the information they choose to summarize. Topics that generate interest or controversy, have social implications, provide solutions to common problems, or deal with mysterious subjects are likely candidates for popular press outlets. Therefore, critical thinkers realize that what appears in the popular press is a biased sample of information from a professional viewpoint. Topics that are not "glitzy" simply are not covered by the popular press. For an example, go to your local bookstore and look at the books in the "psychology" section. It seems that half the books in this section deal with sex—you might come to the conclusion that psychologists are preoccupied with sex. Certainly sex is a legitimate topic for psychologists to study, but it does not comprise such a substantial portion of the discipline.

Fifth, as good critical readers we should be able to track down the original source behind each article in the popular press. The popular writer should provide the reader with clues for locating that original source. Such clues may include the name of the original journal that published the article, the name of the researcher, or the institution where the research was conducted. Any of these leads will enable you to find the original article to evaluate it more carefully and critically, rather than merely accepting the popular writer's words. It is unwise to rely on one person's interpretation of what another person has said or written. This is why, as you may have previously learned, you should avoid secondary citations when you gather information for writing papers.

A Case Study

As you can see, there are good reasons to remain wary of summaries of scientific research that you read in the popular press. Let's look at a specific example of the popular press's handling of a set of scientific findings.

The Star, a widely circulated tabloid (similar to those you may see at the supermarket checkout counter), published an article about research conducted by Dr. Catherine Fichten. According to *The Star*, Fichten had students rate the accuracy or usefulness of horoscopes for the 12 astrological signs. Some students knew which horoscope was actually theirs and some did not. The headline for the article proclaimed "Horoscopes Really True, Says Psychologist" (1983, p. 32). Two quotes from the tabloid article (p. 32) summarized the conclusions from the original article: "Dr. Fichten said the students in both groups rated the horoscopes that matched their birth dates as the most accurate." "Daily and monthly forecasts must have some validity or the subjects would not have rated their own forecasts as more useful than the others, Dr. Fichten said."

American Astrology published an article the following year that was based on the article in *The Star* ("Science and Horoscopes," 1984). The *American Astrology* article stated, "According to an article in the October 11th edition of the tabloid, *The Star,* a psychologist at Dawson College in Montreal has concluded that there is some truth and validity to astrology!" (p. 21). Fichten is also quoted in this second article, although the "quote" appears to be merely lifted directly from *The Star's* article.

Dr. Fichten became aware of the popular press's coverage of her research from a student who had read about Fichten's research in *The Star* and was excited about Fichten's apparent interest in, and support for, astrology (Fichten, 1984). Fichten was amazed at the differences between her research article and the articles in *The Star* and *American Astrology*. Let's look at the original research article to determine what the research actually showed.

Fichten did not conduct her research alone; she had a collaborator. Fichten and Sunerton (1983) conducted an experiment dealing with students' belief in horoscopes. They gave 12 daily horoscope forecasts (from two different sources) to 192 introductory psychology students and had the students rate the usefulness of the forecasts: "How personally useful would this forecast have been for you if you had read it yesterday?" (Fichten & Sunerton, p. 125). Another 150 students performed the same task except that the horoscopes were monthly forecasts (again from two sources) rather than daily. About half the students were told which sign belonged with which forecast and about half were not. Fichten and Sunerton found that students who did not know which daily forecast belonged to which sign did *not* rate the forecast for their sign any more favorably than the average of the 11 other signs. Fichten and Sunerton concluded, "Thus, it appears that daily forecasts were not valid" (p. 128). Likewise, they found that uninformed participants did not find their monthly forecasts to be any more useful than the average for the other signs. Again they concluded that "these results suggest that monthly forecasts were not valid" (p. 128). Not surprisingly, Fichten and Sunerton found that students who knew which forecast was theirs rated that forecast as more personally useful than the remaining 11 forecasts. It seems that participants found horoscopes to be useful only when each horoscope was individually identified. As Fichten and Sunerton pointed out, "When sign is known, as it is in all horoscopes, people may be motivated to ignore predictions that do not fit and to focus on predictions which do" (p. 131). Simply put, people who read and believe horoscopes may be biased in their use of the predictions.

The Star reported fairly accurately about the methods used in collecting the data for the original research. Fichten and Sunerton's conclusions are relatively clear, simple, and straightforward. It is hard to imagine that anyone could read their paper, including the quotes provided here, and misinterpret it. Yet that is exactly what happened. It is clear that the tabloid's statements are exactly opposite of Fichten and Sunerton's conclusions. Both popular press articles also presented the story as though a reporter had interviewed Fichten, but she said that she spoke to no one from the popular press (Fichten, 1984).

Critical Thinking Errors

In Chapter 1, we learned seven guidelines for critical thinkers. Which guidelines were not met in this case about believing horoscopes? The main violation occurred in Guideline 2 (identifying inherent biases and assumptions). The writers and editors of *The Star* and *American Astrology* clearly appear biased in favor of astrology. This bias blinded them to any critical evaluation.

Also, Guideline 7 (examining available evidence before drawing conclusions) was violated. Although the writers and editors may have examined evidence, they revised the evidence to fit their position.

Thinking about Preconceptions

What could happen as a result of this case? If we were biased in favor of astrology, we might read the popular press reports and accept them at face value. This example presents a strong case for the need to avoid secondary citations and references. If you had read only *The Star,* you would come away with an impression of Dr. Fichten's research that would be inaccurate. If the writer at *American Astrology* had consulted the original research article rather than only *The Star,* then an incorrect article would not have been published in that magazine. People who ask critical questions typically avoid taking someone else's word without checking it out. Be prepared to find original research reports and read them so that you can get the whole picture and draw the correct conclusions.

Fichten and Sunerton's evidence is capable of withstanding critical scrutiny. They collected empirical evidence, not opinions or case studies. They employed some important control techniques that allowed them to draw their conclusions. For example, they used horoscopes from two different sources to increase the generalizability of their findings. More importantly, some students read the forecasts blind (they did not know which forecast belonged to which sign), and some read forecasts that were labeled with the correct astrological signs. The result that blind participants did not find their actual forecasts any more useful than the other 11 forecasts is strong evidence against the usefulness of horoscopes. The finding that informed students judged their forecasts to be more useful than the other 11 forecasts gives us some insight into why some people believe in horoscopes.

We should remain cautious about drawing a conclusion based only on the evidence in this chapter. Remember that we want to be careful about drawing a general conclusion from only one study. To draw a more general conclusion about horoscopes, we should look for more research studies concerning that topic. Even scientific studies do not become credible sources until other researchers can demonstrate similar findings—a process referred to as replication.

Conclusion

Is the enduring lesson from this chapter the notion that you should not trust anything you read about psychology in the popular press? No, I do not want to create that type of disdain for media reports about psychology. However, I hope that you will critically analyze and think about psychology as it is reported on and written about in the popular press. An important problem is illustrated by the example in this chapter. On the one hand, if you previously doubted horoscopes and had read one of the popular press articles, you might have used your critical analysis skills and questioned the conclusion. On the other hand, if you believed in horoscopes and are like many people, you might have taken the articles as confirmation of your belief and never questioned them. Remember that as critical thinkers we must keep a skeptical attitude even about ideas with which we agree.

Again, I do not wish to undermine your confidence in everything that you read about psychology. Magazines such as *Time, Newsweek,* and *US News & World Report* are certainly more credible than supermarket tabloids. However, I would argue that it is quite important to keep your healthy skepticism as you read, regardless of the source. Don't accept everything at face value without questioning. People who make various claims should be able to support those claims. Ask for the evidence and evaluate it critically. This attitude of critical inquiry should help make you a much more informed and discriminating consumer of psychological information.

Critical Thinking Challenges

1. Psychology or psychology-related information can be found in almost any type of popular press. Find an article from a newspaper or magazine that deals with some element of psychology. What are your preconceptions about this topic? Analyze this article according to the guidelines for critical thinking provided in Chapter 1. Is this article an example of "good psychology," or is it written in a casual manner from a biased viewpoint? Find the original study referenced in the article to determine whether the article summarized the study fairly and accurately.

2. The example provided in this chapter dealt with the scientific investigation of horoscopes. As I mentioned, one article that determines horoscopes are invalid is not enough to draw a general conclusion about horoscopes. Go to your library and find three more research articles dealing with horoscopes. Using the three articles and the Fichten and Sunerton (1983) study, analyze this area of research using the Chapter 1 critical thinking guidelines. Can you draw a general conclusion from the four studies and support it with evidence?

3. Look at the table of contents in your psychology text. Choose a topic that you will study this term about which you have some preconceived notion. Using the text references as a guide, find three research articles from your library that are relevant to your topic. Write an analysis of your preconceptions and the research article using the Chapter 1 guidelines as a framework.

References

Fichten, C. (1984, May). Beware the press [Letter to the editor]. *APA Monitor,* p. 5.

Fichten, C. S., & Sunerton, B. (1983). Popular horoscopes and the "Barnum" effect. *The Journal of Psychology, 114,* 123–134.

Horoscopes really true, says psychologist. (1983, October 11). *The Star,* p. 32.

Rubenstein, J. (1976). On reading the popular press. In J. Rubenstein (Ed.), *Readings in psychology 76/77* (pp. 2–5). Guilford, CT: Dushkin.

Science and horoscopes. (1984). *American Astrology, 51,* p. 21.

3

🌿

Statistical Seduction

One of the most famous quotes concerning statistics is attributed to Benjamin Disraeli (British prime minister in the 1870s): "There are three kinds of lies: lies, damned lies, and statistics." Although he overstated the case, there is no doubt that people sometimes misuse statistics. The problem that we will deal with in this chapter is statistical seduction—attempts by people to sway or mislead us with statistics. We will learn some of their tricks and focus on critical thinking about statistics.

Huff (1954) wrote an engaging book, *How to Lie with Statistics,* in which he categorized several ways that people attempt to deceive us with numbers. Let's take a look at several of these attempts at deception, using Huff's categories.

The Sample with the Built-in Bias

How often do you hear claims such as "57% of people surveyed use Baby's Derriere talcum powder"? Do you ever wonder 57% of *whom?* This question is a good, critical question to ask about claims made from some unknown sample. Psychologists know that *random samples* should be chosen to best represent the population. A random sample is chosen so that every member of the population has an equal chance of being selected. Any selection method that systematically excludes some people is *biased*. For us to be confident about the talcum powder results, the people surveyed should have been selected randomly. We would feel deceived if we find out that the people surveyed were attending a Baby's Derriere stockholders' meeting!

In a famous case of drawing a conclusion from a biased sample, the *Literary Digest* conducted a poll concerning the 1936 presidential election by mailing 10 million ballots. Their survey, based on over 2 million responses, predicted that Alf Landon would win a landslide election over Franklin Roosevelt. However, Roosevelt won the 1936 election with 61% of the vote (Spatz, 2001). What went wrong? The sample was biased because of the return rate of the survey. Only 23% of the surveys were returned (Paulos, 1988). It is probable that more people who were unhappy with Roosevelt's first term returned the ballots. Paulos (1988) noted that mail surveys are prone to a selection bias—a case in which the people more interested and excited about an issue are more likely to respond to the survey. Before we can be confident about the results of a survey, we need information about the nature of the sample. Biased samples yield biased results that we should ignore. Today's pollsters are careful to draw samples that are near-perfect representatives of the population. Still, in a close election (such as George Bush vs. Al Gore in 2000), it was difficult to make an accurate prediction even with an unbiased sample.

The Little Figures That Are Not There

Using our Baby's Derriere talcum powder example, do you ever wonder *how many* people were surveyed to arrive at the magical 57% figure? This number seems like an odd value, so we might assume that a large number of people were surveyed. Did you realize that 4 out of 7 equals 57%? How impressed would you be to know that 4 out of 7 people surveyed said that they used Baby's Derriere brand? Not terribly, I hope! In order to critically evaluate results from a sample, we need to know how large the sample is.

The size of the sample often is not provided for our scrutiny. A prime example of this problem occurs in commercials. If "four out of five doctors" recommend some product, does this mean that 80% of a large survey of doctors recommended it or that literally 4 of 5 doctors recommended the product? Clearly, the former possibility is much more impressive and is the conclusion that the advertising company hopes that we draw. When I hear such a phrase, my internal "alarm" beeps, and I immediately become suspicious. I hope that you also have such an internal caution indicator. Know the size of the sample before drawing conclusions from that sample.

The Well-Chosen Average

We are inundated with information about averages throughout our lives—batting averages, the average cost of a new home, average salary, and so on. People typically feel comfortable about these statistics because they have computed averages since they were kids in school. Doesn't everyone know how to find the average of a set of numbers? There seems to be no way to make this statistical concept difficult. Wrong! When using statistics, the term *average* is a vague and (perhaps) misleading term. Why? There are actually three statistical averages commonly used—the mean, median, and mode. Psychologists often refer to *central values* or *measures of central tendency* rather than averages.

The *mean* is what you have known for many years as the average. It is simply the arithmetic average of the scores, calculated by adding the scores and dividing the sum by the number of scores. Thus, if your history class produced the set of exam scores shown in Figure 3-1, the mean score would be 66.7 (734 divided by 11).

As you look at that set of exam scores, you see that three students apparently did not study. Their low scores reduced the class mean considerably. A problem with the mean is that it is affected by extreme scores, as in this case. To reduce the impact of extreme scores, we use the median. The *median* is the point that divides a set of scores into two equal parts. A simple way of conceptualizing the median is to think of it as the middle score (when the scores are ordered from highest to lowest) in a distribution of scores. When we arrange our history exam scores

93	
91	
84	
84	
77	
75	Mean = 734/11 = 66.7
71	Median = middle score = 75
66	Mode = 84
32	
31	
30	$n = 11$
734	

Figure 3-1
History Exam Scores

in order (as shown in Figure 3-1), we find that the median is 75 because there are five scores above and below 75. This figure seems like a more reasonable estimate of the "average" performance of the class because it minimizes the negative impact of the people who did not study. (If the number of scores is even, the median is the mean of the two scores in the middle of the distribution.) If you have several "brains" in the class, the median would minimize the impact of their high scores on the central value. By using the median, each extreme score has the same impact as any other score—it merely counts as one score. The *mode* is simply the most frequent score found in a distribution. In Figure 3-1, the mode is 84, a score that two students achieved.

Now we are faced with a dilemma. Which central value should we use? We typically use the mean unless there is a potential problem of misinterpretation in using the mean, such as a distribution that is heavily weighted by scores at either end of the distribution. Such a situation results in a *skewed distribution*. When scores are skewed, the mean is sensitive to the extreme scores, and the median should then be used. Which central value should we use for the history exam scores? Because of the cluster of very low scores, the data appear to be skewed, so we should not use the mean. The mode is not a very useful central value unless we are making frequency counts—for example, how many of your fellow students are Republicans and how many are Democrats? Thus, the median of 75 would be the most appropriate central value to use for this distribution of exam scores.

How can someone attempt to mislead us by using averages? When someone talks about an "average," most people assume that the speaker is referring to a mean, probably because they are familiar only with the mean as a central value. However, the "average" could refer to a mean, median, or mode. Choosing a particular value could help strengthen or weaken the case for the point the person is trying to make. Imagine finding the "average" income of a small community with several rich people. The mean would be inflated by the rich people's incomes. If you wanted the community to appear prosperous, you might use the mean. To make the community eligible for low-income assistance, you might use the median. Both represent the "average" income. However, for *any* skewed distribution (such as income in the United States), you should use the median. The bottom line about central values is fairly simple—whenever you hear the word *average,* your internal statistics alarm should start beeping, and you should ask yourself "*Which* average?"

Much Ado about Practically Nothing

Psychologists use statistics to help make decisions about information from research studies. If the factors they study affect behavior, the results show a significant difference. For example, suppose that you have developed a memory pill; people who take it remember more than people who don't take the pill. You conclude that the drug contained in the pill has a significant effect on memory.

A semantic confusion may mislead us statistically. Results are termed *significant* when statistical tests indicate that it is unlikely that the results occurred by chance. In this situation, *significant* is *not* synonymous with *important*. The importance of results deals with their practical nature—can they can be applied meaningfully to some situation? Suppose the significant difference occurred because people who took the memory pill remembered 1 more word out of a list of 50 than people who did not take the pill. Would this *significant* difference be large enough to be an *important* difference? For example, should all school children take the pill because of its effects? Because *significant* and *important* are often used interchangeably in nonstatistical speech, people who are not statistically sophisticated often assume that these terms are also interchangeable in statistical situations.

It is simple to find results that are statistically significant but that are virtually meaningless in terms of importance, particularly in cases that involve large samples of data. Meehl (1970) wrote about a study of 55,000 Minnesota high school seniors who were measured on 45 different variables. When researchers looked at the associations between all pairings of the variables, 91% of them turned out to be significant, simply because of the large sample. As you might guess, not all of those relationships were important and meaningful.

Don't confuse statistical significance with importance. It is up to the person reporting the statistics to tell you whether they are significant; it is up to you to decide whether statistical differences are important or meaningful in real life.

The Gee-Whiz Graph

Based on an old saying, a picture is worth a thousand words. Psychologists seem to be fond of this saying, as they often present information through graphs. To explain graphical information in words might require the proverbial thousand words. Combining a graph and a verbal explanation gives the best of both worlds. Information is provided for both verbally oriented and visually oriented persons. Presumably, then, almost anyone can understand the information presented.

Researchers should use certain conventions when creating graphs (Spatz, 2001). One convention is that the graph's height should be about two-thirds of its width, which keeps the graph in proportion and helps prevent intentionally misleading someone with a poorly drawn graph. Imagine plotting the data on unmarried couples' households (see Table 3-1) on the two sets of axes shown in Figure 3-2. Can you predict what the two graphs would

Table 3-1
Unmarried Couples' Households, 1960–2000 (in thousands)

1960	1970	1980	1990	2000
439	523	1589	2856	3839

From *Marital Status and Living Arrangements: March 1991,* U.S. Bureau of the Census, 1992, Washington, DC. (Data for 2000 are estimated.)

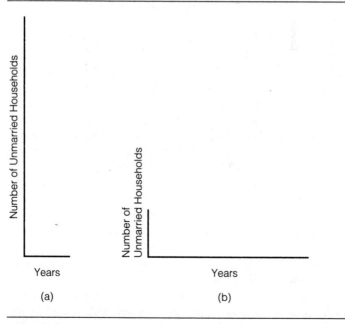

Figure 3-2
Misleading Graphic Axes

appear to show (with the same data plotted)? Which graph would seem to depict very dramatic changes in the data over time? Which graph would seem to show a great degree of stability over time? If you answered graph a to the first question and graph b to the second question, you are thinking critically about graphs. Which data plot would be correct? The answer is neither, because both graphs violate the height-to-width ratio and would, therefore, be misleading. Only when the graph is proportioned correctly can you extract the necessary information from it.

Another graphic strategy that can be misleading involves jumping the scale on one or both axes of the graph without letting the reader know. Jumping the scale is often done because the numbers being graphed are quite large and do not fall close to the origin (the zero point on both axes). Rather than drawing a graph that is very tall or very wide, the convention is to break the axis with slash marks to indicate that part of the graph is missing (Spatz, 2001). Figure 3-3 shows a graph that appeared in the *APS Observer,* a publication of the American Psychological Society. When you glance at the graph, what impression do you get? Is APS membership growing rapidly or slowly? Now study the graph more carefully. What is wrong with this graph? You probably notice that the number of members scale on the graph jumped considerably with no slash marks to indicate the jump. Thus, a change of about 4000 people comprises the majority of the graph whereas the base of over 6000 people was condensed into a fraction of the space devoted to the change. This graph appears to be drawn in a misleading fashion to give the impression that APS was growing more rapidly than it actually was.

When we look at graphs, we need to examine them carefully. Our task is to extract the information that is condensed in the graph. Before we can extract the information, we should be certain that the graph presents the information accurately. Don't be misled by a graph that is drawn to prove a point.

The Semiattached Figure

People who want to convince us of their position often confront us with statistics to buttress their argument. Sometimes the numbers cited are not relevant. I am reminded of an aspirin commercial that touted its product as being absorbed into the bloodstream very quickly. This is a perfect example of the semiattached figure. We become caught up in the absorption rate of the aspirin and forget to ask whether the product actu-

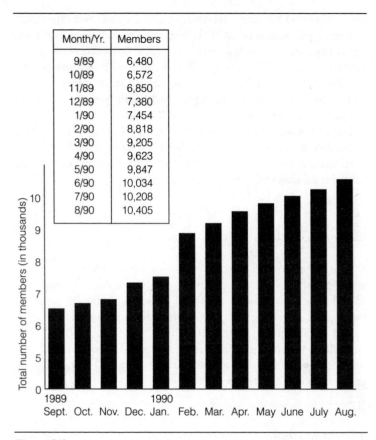

Month/Yr.	Members
9/89	6,480
10/89	6,572
11/89	6,850
12/89	7,380
1/90	7,454
2/90	8,818
3/90	9,205
4/90	9,623
5/90	9,847
6/90	10,034
7/90	10,208
8/90	10,405

Figure 3-3
Membership Statistics for the American Psychological Society
From the *American Psychological Society Observer, 1990,* p. 10.

ally *works!* An aspirin that is absorbed instantaneously is still not very good if it does not provide pain relief. In this case, the semiattached figure looks and sounds impressive, but it is not really the main issue. Many advertisers attempt to divert our attention by playing on side issues in their ads.

Correlation and Causality

This last statistical problem is not one that Huff (1954) listed, but it is quite problematic, sometimes even for people who present data. Although it may be common sense to assume that two correlated variables are involved in a cause-and-effect relationship, that assumption is wrong. Correlation does *not* imply causality. Many studies have shown a correlation between watching violent TV and aggression, but this relationship does not allow us to conclude that watching violence *causes* aggressive behavior. Aggressive people could simply prefer to watch violent shows, or some third variable (such as a hormonal imbalance) could lead to both violence and a tendency to watch such shows. So, if you hear someone conclude that one variable causes another because the two variables are correlated, you should detect the flaw in that reasoning.

Critical Thinking Errors

Which errors in critical thinking show up in this chapter? Misleading statistics show a problem with Guideline 6 (using logical inference processes). Statistical reasoning is based on drawing logical inferences, so misleading through statistics is often based on illogical inferences. There is also a problem with Guideline 4 (separating facts from opinions). People may try to mislead you with faulty statistics (their opinions) if they cannot present accurate statistics (facts).

Thinking about Preconceptions

In this chapter I have shown you seven different ways that people might attempt to mislead you with statistics. You probably don't have preconceived notions about all seven of these areas.

The general preconception that you need to beware of is an awe of statistics. Because many people are intimidated by numbers, they do not think critically about statistics. You will be faced with numbers throughout your life—not just in psychology and not just in college. If you simply "roll over and play dead" when someone confronts you with statistics, you have given that person an advantage over you. Thinking critically about numerical arguments is similar to thinking critically about verbal arguments—you simply have to remember to apply your critical analysis skills rather than give up because numbers are involved.

Conclusion

The author of a well-known statistics text warned me to be careful in writing this chapter. He admonished me to explain it as I went along or "otherwise they will conclude that 'statistics can be used to prove anything' which is YUCK" (C. Spatz, personal communication, May 19, 1993). I hope that I have not given you the impression that statistics can be used to prove anything *or* that statistics can't be used to prove anything. I do hope that I *have* convinced you that you should not ignore statistics or hide your head when they are used. In this chapter I have given you some tools for critically examining statistics. Don't be afraid of statistics! Statistics are used to provide clearer evidence for arguments. Because statistics often form the backbone of psychological arguments, it is important for you to subject them to critical analysis and thought.

Critical Thinking Challenges

1. Suppose you want to conduct a survey of students at your school regarding their opinion of the U.S. president's job performance.
   a. Further suppose that you are employed by the Republican Re-election Committee, so you want the survey to yield favorable results. What method(s) could you use to draw a biased sample of students that would be likely to rate the president highly?
   b. Suppose instead that you are employed by the Democratic Election Committee and would like to collect unfavorable results. What method(s) could you use to draw a sample biased against the president?
   c. What method(s) would you use to draw a fair (unbiased) sample of students from your school for this survey?
2. No baseball player has batted over .400 since the 1941 baseball season. After 40 games of the 162 game baseball season, William Tedds is batting .406. Sportswriters are writing articles about how Tedds will make baseball history by batting .400 for the year. What is the statistical flaw in their reasoning?
3. Which measure of central tendency should be used for each of the following sets of data? Why? Provide a compelling rationale for each case.

a. The average cost of all new homes built in the United States
b. The typical brand of toothbrush used
c. The average cost of heating (or cooling) a home
d. The average monthly food bill for a family of four
e. The most popular car for college students

4. You are serving as a student member on your school's admissions committee. You are considering two students, but there is room at the college for only one. Student A has an ACT score of 24, and student B has an ACT score of 23. The registrar argues long and hard for admitting student A because it is obvious that student A is more intelligent. How do you respond to the registrar?

5. Find a graph published in a newspaper or magazine. Do you spot any flaws in it? If so, what are they? What impression does the artist hope you will draw? Is that impression the correct conclusion to draw? If you find the graph to be flawed, redraw it so that the correct conclusion is more readily apparent.

6. Suppose you heard the following statement on the TV news: "The number of passengers killed in airline crashes last year was up 17%. People are becoming more afraid of flying and are changing their travel plans to trains, buses, and automobiles. Congress is beginning a probe into airline safety." Your friend, watching the news with you, is cheered by this news, believing that airplanes are unsafe. How do you respond to your friend and to the news report?

References

Huff, D. (1954). *How to lie with statistics*. New York: Norton.

Meehl, P. E. (1970). Theory testing in psychology and physics: A methodological paradox. In D. E. Morrison & R. E. Henkel (Eds.), *The significance test controversy: A reader* (pp. 252–266). Chicago: Aldine.

Paulos, J. A. (1988). *Innumeracy: Mathematical illiteracy and its consequences*. New York: Hill and Wang.

Spatz, C. (2001). *Basic statistics: Tales of distributions* (7th ed.). Belmont, CA: Wadsworth.

4

❦

Anatomy Is Destiny—Or Is It?

One interesting debate in psychology deals with gender differences. Extensive literature reviews have confirmed that gender differences do exist, although they are typically small differences (see Figure 4-1) and appear to be decreasing over time (Basow, 1992). Standard gender differences uncovered by research include: (1) males are more aggressive, (2) females have superior verbal ability, (3) males have superior mathematical ability, and (4) males have superior visual-spatial ability (Maccoby & Jacklin, 1974). Also, (5) males are more active, (6) males are more competitive (after puberty), (7) females are slightly more compliant, and (8) males are dominant in selfish ways but females are dominant in communal situations (Basow, 1992). Basow notes that differences in gender roles are ·culturally universal and virtually constant across different cultures—"in most cultures, males primarily are responsible for hunting, fishing, and warfare, and females for gathering foods, cooking, and child care" (1992, p. 106). Thus, the question we will examine in this chapter is not *whether* gender differences exist, but *why* they exist.

Explanations of gender differences typically fall into environmental (e.g., social roles, culture) or hereditary (e.g., hormones, chemistry) possibilities. Because this chapter corresponds to the biological psychology chapter in your text, we will take a very narrow look at only one specific type of biological/physiological explanation for gender differences: differences in brain anatomy. All biological or physiological explanations of gender differences have one common thread—they imply that such differences are unchangeable and immutable. The peril in this assumption is the implication that gender differences are permanently fixed so that changes in society will

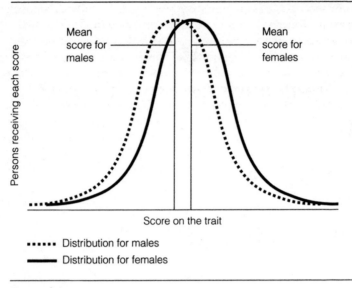

Figure 4-1
Typical Sex Difference Findings

have no impact on them. For people who believe in equality of the sexes and that any differences are due simply to cultural and environmental effects, this immutability would be a dismal prospect. Those who believe in gender equality argue that biological and physiological explanations of gender differences can simply preserve the status quo—if people believe such explanations, they may decide that it is fruitless to work toward changing gender roles. Thus, biological and physiological explanations of gender differences (and other differences as well) have been summarized by the phrase "biology is destiny."

Historically, there have been three approaches to studying the brain that have touched on the topic of gender differences, at least indirectly.

Phrenology

In the early 1800s, scientists began to believe that different functions might be localized in specific areas of the brain. One of the earliest localization doctrines was phrenology, popularized by Gall and Spurzheim (Pogliano, 1991). Phrenologists believed that people who possessed a high level of a certain trait had brains that were overdeveloped in an area corresponding to that trait. Phrenologists "read" the bumps on people's heads to discern their traits. According to Spurzheim, men possessed larger frontal lobes than women; this difference meant that men had greater reflective abilities compared with their perceptive abilities, but the reverse was true of women. Thus, Spurzheim gave "scientific" credence to the stereotypes of men as thinkers and women as perceivers (Shields, 1975). Using one's belief system to justify a stereotype is certainly not a model for critical thinking.

Craniometry

Paul Broca, a French surgeon, was the chief proponent of craniometry, or measurement of the skull (Gould, 1980). Broca believed that the size of one's head could be used as a measure of the size of one's brain, which could be used as a measure of intelligence. Broca performed many autopsies in Paris hospitals and found a mean weight of 1325 grams for 292 male brains compared to a mean of 1144 grams for 140 female brains (Gould, 1980). Thus, he concluded that men are more intelligent. Broca knew, of course, that height differences existed between men and women but he did not believe that physical size alone could account for the difference in brain weight. In 1861, Broca wrote,

> We must not forget that women are, on the average, a little less intelligent than men, a difference which we should not exaggerate but which is, nonetheless, real. We are therefore permitted to suppose that the relatively small size of the female brain depends in part upon her physical inferiority and in part upon her intellectual inferiority. (quoted in Gould, 1980, p. 154)

Notice the circular logic here. Broca reasoned that physical differences alone could not account for the brain difference because of the preexisting supposition that females are intellectually inferior. However, he failed to remember that the intellectual difference between males and females was the original question under scrutiny!

Inevitably, this conclusion led to justifications for discrimination against women, even from the scientific community. Gustave Le Bon, a leading scientist and a founder of social psychology, was particularly malicious in his attacks on women based on Broca's data (Gould, 1980). He compared women's brains to those of gorillas and referred to women as closer to children and savages than to adult, civilized males. Le Bon believed that women lacked the capacity for thought and reason. In 1879, Le Bon wrote, "Without doubt there exist some distinguished women, very superior to the average man, but they are as exceptional as the birth of any monstrosity, as, for example, of a gorilla with two heads; consequently, we may neglect them entirely" (quoted in Gould, 1980, p. 155). Again, we see people using their "science" to perpetuate their belief system and stereotyping.

Brain Localization

As science developed more precise ways to study the brain, researchers began to look closely at particular areas of the brain, based on the assumption that particular abilities are located in the same relative position in everyone's brain. The study of localization continues in a highly refined fashion today, and information from these studies allows us to denote centers of language, vision, movement, planning, and so on. The early days of studying brain localization did not yield such precise data, of course. In the mid-1800s, the frontal lobes were thought to be the seat of intellect, and scientists reported finding larger frontal lobes in males, even in unborn fetuses (Shields, 1975).

By 1900, scientific consensus had changed, and the parietal lobes became regarded as the locale for intelligence. Did scientific opinion now shift to favor females as more intelligent than males? Of course not—the scientific "evidence" itself simply changed. In 1895, G. T. W. Patrick wrote that

> the frontal region is not, as has been supposed, smaller in
> woman, but rather larger relatively. . . . But the parietal lobe is
> somewhat smaller, [furthermore,] a preponderance of the frontal
> region does not imply intellectual superiority . . . the parietal
> region is really the more important. (quoted in Shields, 1975,
> p. 741)

From this example, it is apparent that scientific "evidence" was being used merely to explain or justify stereotypes of male/ female differences rather than to determine the truth about such differences and their origins. Thus, it is clear that brain scientists of the 1800s did not show great evidence of the characteristics of critical thinking we are studying.

Let's jump from the 1800s to the present to examine what we know about localized anatomical gender differences in the brain today. Research has focused on three types of male/female brain differences: laterality, corpus callosum, and hypothalamus.

Laterality

Psychologists generally refer to language as being localized in the left hemisphere and visual-spatial abilities as being right-hemisphere functions, although there are some exceptions. There is some evidence that males are more strongly lateralized than females (Springer & Deutsch, 1998). In other words, males are likely to show the left/language and right/visual-spatial distinction, whereas these abilities are more bilaterally represented in females. Thus, a larger portion of females would have language and visual-spatial abilities localized in both hemispheres rather than in only one. One example of supporting evidence is the fact that males are three times more likely than females to have language disturbances after left-hemisphere damage such as epilepsy or stroke (Springer & Deutsch, 1998).

However, not all evidence supports the male/lateralized–female/bilateral dichotomy. Kimura (1992) reported that language disturbances are more common in men when damage occurs to the posterior left hemisphere but more common in women when the anterior left hemisphere is damaged. Kimura also found that right-hemisphere damage had no greater effect on visual-spatial ability in men than in women. These data imply that males are no more lateralized than females but that the sexes may have different sites for some localized functions.

Corpus Callosum

De Lacoste-Utamsing & Holloway (1982) reported finding gender differences in the corpus callosum, the bundle of nerve fibers connecting the two hemispheres of the brain. They found that the posterior portion of the corpus callosum (the splenium) was larger in women than in men in their sample of 14 autopsied brains (5 women, 9 men). They have replicated this finding in two additional studies. Because the splenium transfers visual information between brain hemispheres, de Lacoste-Utamsing and Holloway conjectured that women have more bilateral representation of visual-spatial function. If we can assume that a larger corpus callosum indicates more nerve pathways between the hemispheres, then this finding would provide an anatomical basis for women being more bilaterally oriented.

Again, the finding of a larger splenium in women is not without controversy. One later study with a large sample (146 participants) revealed no difference in the size of the splenium but a difference in its shape for men and women (Allen, Richey, Chai, & Gorsky, 1991). Other research (Witelson, 1989, 1995) showed no splenium difference between men and women when body size was taken into account, but a larger isthmus (an area just in front of the splenium) in women. Thus, we are again faced with mixed findings regarding gender and brain anatomy.

Hypothalamus

Following up on animal research, Swaab and Fliers (1985) found human gender differences in one of four small nuclei of the anterior hypothalamus, with men showing this nucleus about 2.5 times larger than women. This area plays a role in sexual behavior of animal species, so it was not surprising to find gender differences here.

Subsequent research about these nuclei in the hypothalamus has been anything but clear. Allen, Hines, Shryne, and Gorski (1989) reported finding that two of the four hypothalamic nuclei were larger in men, but neither was the same difference that Swaab and Fliers (1985) found. LeVay (1991) found only one of those nuclei to be larger in men. Thus, it appears that there *may* be a gender difference in size of one or more nuclei in the anterior hypothalamus, but we cannot be certain about this conclusion and are particularly unclear about which nuclei are different sizes.

These three current areas of research into gender-related brain differences are not meant to exhaust the full range of ongoing studies. It is possible that other brain differences between men and women will be found in the future that are not controversial. These three areas, however, seem representative of this type of research at the present time.

Critical Thinking Errors

Several errors in critical thinking are apparent in this chapter. The major problem is with Guideline 2 (identifying inherent biases). The early brain scientists assumed that men were superior to women and set out to document this superiority. Along the way, they violated Guideline 4 (separating facts from opinions) and Guideline 5 (avoiding oversimplification). If facts got in the way of their opinions, they merely changed or reinterpreted the facts.

Errors in critical thinking may not be as obvious for the more recent research attempting to document brain differences between men and women. Any thinking errors will come from the interpretation of those findings. If brain scientists have a difficult time even agreeing on which brain differences exist between men and women, anyone who concludes that gender differences are rooted in brain differences is guilty of violating Guideline 4 (separating facts from opinions). The factual data simply do not yet exist to even document the differences, much less to conclude what those differences mean. As current evidence shows us, it appears that it will be difficult to find obvious physical discrepancies that can account for behavioral differences between males and females. Also, we cannot overlook the point that even variables such as culture can affect physical development.

Thinking about Preconceptions

It appears that the phrenologists, craniometricians, and early brain localists may have been guilty of operating on preconceived notions. Their "findings" about gender differences in the brain consistently supported the notion of male superiority. It is difficult to know whether preconceptions have contributed to today's mixed findings on male/female brain anatomy differences. Marshall has pointed out that reading tissue slides to determine the size of brain structures is a subjective process: "Results can be affected by the patient's age, type of disease, differences in therapy, speed of death, methods of tissue fixation, and other factors—many of which are undetermined" (1992, p. 621).

How about you? Do you hold preconceptions about the origins of gender differences? Do you believe that differences between males and females are fixed and unchangeable or that

they can evolve over time? The more important question, however, is whether you allow your preconceptions to influence
your evaluation of the evidence. If you choose to believe only
the evidence that supports your position and dismiss the other
side, you are not engaging in critical thinking and analysis. Remember that we must not let our biases color our judgments.

Conclusion

This has been a problematic chapter to write. It is difficult sift-
ing through voluminous research findings that seem to directly
contradict each other. It is especially difficult to write about a
topic that has political ramifications, with a possibility of offend-
ing one group or the other. However, controversial issues such
as gender differences cry out for critical thinking. Too often, in
dealing with controversial topics, people resort to emotional arguments rather than clear, rational thought. When people argue
from emotion, it is difficult to resolve anything. Arguments concerning gender differences often spring from emotion rather
than scientific data. If you can apply the critical thinking guidelines to controversial issues, you can better analyze the issues
and make informed decisions.

The research into the root of gender differences is so
murky at this time that it is difficult to make a clear decision.
However, such a "conclusion" is not a cop-out. The ability to
think critically does not guarantee that you will always reach a
definitive, clear-cut conclusion. Critical thinking does, however,
give you the ability to survey the available evidence and, on certain occasions, decide that it is simply not possible to resolve an
issue. Remember Guideline 1—be tolerant of ambiguity and uncertainty. Gender differences in the brain is one of those issues
that seems impossible to resolve at this time.

Critical Thinking Challenges

1. This chapter revolves around the assumption that gender
   differences occur because of biological factors— thus, "biology is destiny." Derive a detailed counterargument to
   this notion of biological causation of gender differences.
   Give an example that fits your alternative model, and ex-

plain how it supports your notion of causation rather than a biological explanation.

2. What common thread was shared by phrenology, craniometry, and early attempts at brain localization? Why do you think these three approaches had this commonality? What points might these approaches be used to support today?
3. What is the problem with using the male/lateralized–female/bilateral dichotomy to explain both male superiority in visual-spatial ability *and* female superiority in verbal ability?
4. Assume that you are the Director of Brain Research in the United States. You have been given the assignment of reconciling the contradictory findings about gender differences in brain anatomy. What is your strategy? How do you proceed?
5. Choose a behavioral difference between males and females that you believe to be biological in nature. Go to the library and find the available evidence concerning this difference. Does your conclusion match your preconception? What new information did you learn?

References

Allen, L. S., Hines, M., Shryne, J. E., & Gorski, R. A. (1989). Two sexually dimorphic cell groups in the human brain. *Journal of Neuroscience, 9,* 497–506.

Allen, L. S., Richey, M. F., Chai, Y. M., & Gorski, R. A. (1991). Sex differences in the corpus callosum of the living human being. *Journal of Neuroscience, 11,* 933–942.

Basow, S. A. (1992). *Gender: Stereotypes and roles* (3rd ed.). Pacific Grove, CA: Brooks/Cole.

de Lacoste-Utamsing, C., & Holloway, R. L. (1982). Sexual dimorphism in the human corpus callosum. *Science, 216,* 1431–1432.

Gould, S. J. (1980). *The panda's thumb: More reflections in natural history.* New York: Norton.

Kimura, D. (1992, September). Sex differences in the brain. *Scientific American,* pp. 119–125.

LeVay, S. (1991). A difference in hypothalamic structure between heterosexual and homosexual men. *Science, 253,* 1034–1037.

Maccoby, E. E., & Jacklin, C. N. (1974). *The psychology of sex differences.* Stanford, CA: Stanford University Press.

Marshall, E. (1992). Sex on the brain. *Science, 257,* 620–621.

Pogliano, C. (1991). Between form and function: A new science of man. In P. Corsi (Ed.), *The enchanted loom: Chapters in the history of neuroscience* (pp. 144–157). New York: Oxford University Press.

Shields, S. A. (1975). Functionalism, Darwinism, and the psychology of women: A study in social myth. *American Psychologist, 30,* 739–754.

Springer, S. P., & Deutsch, G. (1998). *Left brain, right brain* (5th ed.). New York: W. H. Freeman.

Swaab, D. F., & Fliers, E. (1985). A sexually dimorphic nucleus in the human brain. *Science, 228,* 1112–1115.

Witelson, S. F. (1989). Hand and sex differences in the isthmus and genu of the human corpus callosum. *Brain, 112,* 799–835.

Witelson, S. F. (1995). Neuroanatomical bases of hemispheric functional specialization in the human brain: Possible developmental factors. In F. L. Kitterle (Ed.), *Hemispheric communication: Mechanisms and models* (pp. 61–84). Hillsdale, NJ: Erlbaum.

5

Is What You See What You Get?

Many people believe that perception works like a video or audio recorder, simply recording images for later playback so we can identify what we saw or heard. Thus, we would receive information in our environment at face value and act on that information. This intuitive perceptual theory is easy to understand and quite appealing. It is so simple and appealing, in fact, that some computer companies advertise their programs as WYSIWYG ("what you see is what you get"). These programs allow users to print documents that duplicate exactly what is displayed on the computer screen.

A WYSIWYG-like approach to perception formed the cornerstone for early perceptual theories. Bruner and Goodman (1947, p. 33) noted that such theories assume the perceiver is "a passive recording instrument" who could be described in terms used "to describe the latest piece of recording apparatus available." In this model, perception (the label) is a product of the properties of the stimulus—what you see (the stimulus) is what you get (your perception). In perceptual terms, *stimulus variables* (aspects of the actual stimulus) dictate what you see. In this chapter, we'll evaluate this preconception about perception.

It should be clear that stimulus variables *do* affect perception. Aspects of a stimulus such as its color, size, clarity, and distance from you certainly affect how accurately you perceive the stimulus. However, is this simple theory enough to account for all our perceptions? If you have ever experienced a perceptual illusion, you know the answer to this question is "No." When we experience illusions, what we see is *not* what we get—our perception does not match the stimulus. Interestingly though, the perception becomes our reality, regardless of the stimulus that is actually present. In other words, what we perceive to be reality may be a distorted or biased view of reality. Therefore, we need to discover what kinds of variables can cause us to experience distorted perceptions. Would you believe that one major factor is organismic variables—factors within you?

Organismic Variables

Stop for a moment and help me with the following demonstration. I want you to say the alphabet aloud as quickly as you can, making sure that each letter can be clearly understood. (I'm waiting. . . . Please humor me for a few seconds.) After you have finished reciting the alphabet, turn the page and look at Figure 5-1. What do you see? If you are like many people, you will have perceived the letter *B*. Suppose I ask you to count to 20 before looking at Figure 5-1. What do you then perceive? Probably the number *13*. Hmmm . . . isn't that interesting? You saw the same stimulus in both cases and it stimulated the cells in your retina in the same manner both times. Yet your perceptions were different in the two situations. How could this occur? The difference, of course, was the context provided for the stimulus. When you recited the alphabet, that context made you more likely to decide you had seen a letter. In contrast, having you count gave you a number context. The context induced a perceptual set within you. A *perceptual set* prepares you to perceive things in a certain way.

You may have noticed that it was more difficult to perceive the object in Figure 5-1 as *13* than as *B*. That difficulty occurred because you first perceived the object as a letter. Once a perceptual set has been established, it is often difficult to change. For example, look at Figure 5-2. What do you see? Although this is a well-known reversible figure, many people have difficulty seeing it reverse. If you see an old woman with a large nose looking to the left, you may have trouble seeing a young woman facing away from you, and vice versa. Every time I show this figure in class, some students never manage to see both images. Once they have perceived the figure in a certain way, they are not able to overcome their perceptual set to perceive anything else. Thus, previous experience with a stimulus item *(priming)* can establish a perceptual set within an individual. The importance of a perceptual set is that it shows a factor within the observer, not merely the stimulus it-self, that can alter perception. Have you ever "heard" scary noises in your house after staying up late to watch a horror movie? The movie primed you to be afraid of noises that would not have alarmed you if you had watched a funny movie. Al-though a friend may try to convince you that these noises are merely typical noises in the house, your distorted perception becomes the "reality" of danger (see Figure 5-3 for a humorous example).

Expectations

Let's look at some other variables that can induce a perceptual set within an observer. Expectations play a powerful role in de-termining perceptions. How many times have you had the ex-perience of proofreading your term paper over and over for ty-pographical errors, feeling certain that you have caught all the typos, and having your teacher spot an error almost as soon as you turned the paper in? This is a good example of the power of expectation coloring our perception. Your perception of no errors is a product not merely of the stimulus, but also of your expectations—you don't detect any errors because you know what the paper is supposed to say. When you proofread the pa-per, those expectations influenced your perception. Have you ever noticed that cooks trying new recipes do not want to tell you the ingredients until *after* you have tasted the food so that you don't fall victim to expectation effects? Because I dislike mushrooms, my wife will never tell me when she puts mush-rooms in something she cooks! If I knew a dish contained mush-rooms, my perception of it would be distorted in a negative fashion.

Similar expectation effects have been found in research on touch perception. Meyer, Gross, and Teuber (1963) touched various locations on participants' hands, either with or without alerting the people where they were going to be touched. The researchers found that when participants knew where they were to be touched (expectation present), they could detect lighter touches than when they had no expectation. You would prob-ably be highly accurate at detecting your typos in your term pa-pers if you knew which words you were going to misspell! Ex-pectations definitely distort our perceptions.

В

Figure 5-1
What Do You Perceive?

From *Inversions,* by Scott Kim. Copyright © 1989 Scott Kim. Used with permission of W. H. Freeman and Company.

Figure 5-2
Who Do You See?

From "A New Ambiguous Figure," by E. G. Boring, 1930, *American Journal of Psychology, 42,* 444–445. Copyright © 1930 by the Board of Trustees of the University of Illinois Press.

Figure 5-3
Priming Effect in Horror Movies
Reprinted with special permission of King Feature Syndicate.

Learning

Learning is another organismic variable that affects our perceptions. Information we have learned affects the way that we perceive the world around us. One important way that learning affects us is that it provides a context within which we process and perceive information. Right now, where you are sitting, can you imagine the smell of a hospital or dentist's office? Did you feel a small shiver run down your spine when you imagined the smell? Learning has influenced your interpretation of that odor—it was meaningless to you until you associated the smell with the typically unpleasant things that happen at the hospital or dentist's office.

Palmer (1975) showed the importance of context in an item perception task. Figure 5-4 shows sample stimuli from Palmer's experiment. Participants saw a slide such as the left of Figure 5-4 for two seconds followed by a very brief presentation of one of the three slides (a, b, or c) shown on the right. The task was simply to identify the object shown in the second slide. Notice, in Figure 5-4, how the bread (a) is relevant to the context of the earlier slide (kitchen) but the mailbox (b) and drum (c) are not. Participants were almost twice as accurate at identifying objects following a relevant context (83%) than those following an irrelevant context (44%). Perception was an easier task after priming with a context made relevant through learning.

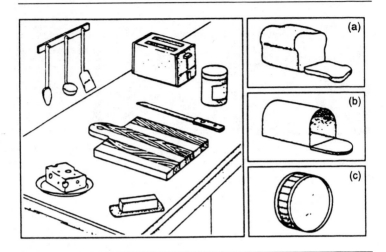

Figure 5-4
Stimuli from Palmer's (1975) Experiment
From "The Effects of Contextual Scenes on the Identification of Objects," by
S. E. Palmer, 1975, *Memory and Cognition, 3,* 519–526. Copyright © 1975.
Reprinted by permission of Psychonomic Society, Inc.

Motivation

Another factor that can distort our perceptions is motivation. Certain conditions can motivate us to perceive certain things in our environment or to perceive our environment in certain ways. Remember watching a ballgame with someone who is rooting for a different team than you? You are watching the same game with the same decisions being made by the same officials, but you disagree vigorously over those decisions. For example, your friend may think the referee has just made the best call of his life while you believe that the ref needs to have his eyes examined. Here, your perceptions (and those of your friend) are influenced by your motivation—your devotion to your team. Have you ever noticed how much better the officials seem when the game you are watching does not involve your favorite team? Do you really think that the officials call a better game in that situation, or might this effect be due to the fact that your motivation in this case is rather low? Let's take a closer look at some perceptual research that shows the influence of motivation.

Several experiments have tested the effect of hunger on perception. Sanford conducted two experiments in which he showed words and pictures to children (1936) and college students (1937) and had the participants give associations to the words and interpretations of the pictures. In both experiments Sanford found that people who had eaten less recently gave more food-related responses to the stimuli. In a similar experiment, McClelland and Atkinson (1948) showed navy men a series of dimly lit slides and asked them to describe what they saw. Sailors who had not eaten for either 4 or 16 hours reported seeing more food-related items and activities than men who had eaten 1 hour earlier. Thus, it seems that hunger motivation "helps" us to perceive things related to food when presented with ambiguous stimuli. Once again, distorted perceptions become "reality."

Bruner and Goodman (1947) studied a different aspect of motivation when they examined children's perception of the size of coins. Ten-year-old children viewed either coins or cardboard circles the same sizes as the coins and then were asked to adjust a circle of light until it was the same size as the stimuli. The children were quite accurate at matching the size of the cardboard stimuli but overestimated the size of coins by 15% to 35%. Bruner and Goodman speculated that value placed on the coins by the children caused them to overestimate the coins' sizes. When Bruner and Goodman divided the children sizing the coins into "rich" and "poor" groups (based on the children's neighborhood), they found that the poor children overestimated the size of the coins by a greater margin. It seems, then, that the higher the level of motivation regarding the stimuli, the greater the effect it had on perception.

Lambert, Solomon, and Watson (1949) followed up Bruner and Goodman's research and showed that perception could be made dependent on a combination of motivation and learning. They had children (ages 3 to 5) adjust a circle of light to match the size of a poker chip. Half the children earned poker chips they could trade for candy by performing the task; the other half received candy directly for working on the task. The children who learned to value the poker chips gave larger size estimates for the chips than children who received candy directly. Once the children had learned that the stimuli were valuable, they perceived them as larger. Interestingly, when the experimenters ceased giving the children candy for the poker chips, the estimates of the chips' size decreased to the same as the group who attached no value to the chips. Clearly the size perception effect was tied to the value of the stimulus.

Critical Thinking Errors

Using a WYSIWYG approach to perception violates Guideline 5 (avoiding oversimplification). Believing that perception works like a copy machine or a camera taking snapshots leaves no room for individualistic coloring of perceptions. Deciding that perception is dependent on both stimulus and organismic variables requires Guideline 7 (examining available evidence before drawing conclusions). Remember to avoid looking for evidence that favors only one side of an argument!

Thinking about Preconceptions

Is what we see what we get? The various forms of a perceptual set covered in this chapter (priming, expectations, learning, motivation) support the notion that organismic variables do affect perception—information within us influences our interpretation of "what is out there." Perception is often influenced in this manner, so the view that perception is merely a product of what we see (or hear, or feel, or smell, or taste) is rather simplistic. To fully explain our perceptions, we must take a multitude of internal factors into account.

Yet, does it make sense to conclude that only internal variables affect our perception? Surely we cannot eliminate factors that involve the actual stimulus! Just as it seems foolish to maintain that observer variables play no role in perception, it would be equally foolish to conclude that the object that is being seen, heard, smelled, tasted, or felt does not enter into the perceptual process. We must process stimulus information so that there will be some basic material to act on. Perception is typically a combination of both processes acting simultaneously. As we encounter our world, we are constantly carrying with us memories of events in the past. Various events we encounter may set up expectations, motives, or other perceptual sets within us. When we first notice a stimulus in our environment, organismic variables interact with the information that we extract from the stimulus itself to form our full-blown perception. In this case, our preconceptions are partially correct.

Conclusion

In this chapter, we have learned a funny thing about critical thinking—it often does not involve simply weighing the evidence concerning two conflicting sides and choosing the side with more evidence in its favor. Two opposing viewpoints are often reconciled by some type of compromise. It seems that just such a compromise is necessary concerning perception. Neither stimulus variables nor organismic variables *alone* can fully explain how we perceive our environment. When we realize that both components contribute to the mechanism of perception, we end up with an explanation that seems to work well.

Critical Thinking Challenges

1. Is it possible to have an example of perception that fits *only* the WYSIWYG approach to processing? If so, what feature(s) must be present for this type of processing to occur alone? If not, why not?
2. Suppose that only stimulus variables affected perception. What would your sense of perception be like? How would this affect the way that you interact with your environment?
3. Think of an episode in your experience where you perceived something other than the stimulus that was actually present. This is an example of organismic variables affecting your perception. Explain the circumstances that caused something other than the stimulus itself to change your perception.
4. Develop a list of five foods that you could color in some odd way (for example, green scrambled eggs, blue mashed potatoes). Ask five friends to rate each of these colored foods on a scale from 1 (*disgusting*) to 10 (*yummy*). Compute the mean for each of the five foods. Look at the lowest-rated and highest-rated foods. Generate a hypothesis for each of these ratings—what organismic variables seem to make one odd-colored food more appetizing than the other?

Figure 5-5
What Do You Perceive?

From "The Role of Frequency in Developing Perceptual Sets," by B. R. Bugelski and D. A. Alampay, 1961, *Canadian Journal of Psychology, 15,* 205–211. Copyright © 1961 Canadian Psychological Association. Reprinted by permission.

5. Look at Figure 5-5. What do you perceive? This is another example of a figure that can be interpreted in more than one manner (as either a rat or a man). What stimulus variables in the figure influenced your perception? What organismic variables influenced your perception? Show the figure to some friends until you find someone who perceives it differently from you. Ask this friend questions so that you can develop a list of stimulus and organismic variables that influenced this person to have a perception different from yours.

References

Bruner, J. S., & Goodman, C. C. (1947). Value and need as organizing factors in perception. *Journal of Abnormal and Social Psychology, 42,* 33–44.

Lambert, W. W., Solomon, R. L., & Watson, D. P. (1949). Reinforcement and extinction as factors in size estimation. *Journal of Experimental Psychology, 39,* 637–641.

McClelland, D. C., & Atkinson, J. W. (1948). The projective expression of needs: I. The effect of different intensities of the hunger drive on perception. *The Journal of Psychology, 25,* 205–222.

Meyer, V., Gross, C. G., & Teuber, H.-L. (1963). Effect of knowledge of site of stimulation on the threshold for pressure sensitivity. *Perceptual and Motor Skills, 16,* 637–640.

Palmer, S. E. (1975). The effects of contextual scenes on the identification of objects. *Memory & Cognition, 3,* 519–526.

Sanford, R. N. (1936). The effects of abstinence from food upon imaginal processes: A preliminary experiment. *The Journal of Psychology, 2,* 129–136.

Sanford, R. N. (1937). The effects of abstinence from food upon imaginal processes: A further experiment. *The Journal of Psychology, 3,* 145–159.

6

🌾

Can Hypnosis Help Me Remember?

If you are typical of most people, you sometimes have trouble remembering information. One alleged benefit of hypnosis is that it can help people recall forgotten information, a phenomenon known as *hypermnesia*. Loftus (1980) found that about 75% of people she surveyed agreed with this statement: "Everything we learn is permanently stored in the mind, although sometimes particular details are not accessible. With hypnosis, or other special techniques, these inaccessible details could eventually be recovered" (p. 43). Wolberg (1982) opened his book on hypnosis with the following story:

> An amnesia victim bewilderedly wanders into the emergency
> department of a public hospital. A few words by a skilled intern
> who has induced hypnosis, and he resumes the broken thread
> of his existence. (p. 3)

Wow! If hypnosis can help someone who seems to have lost all his memories, it certainly should help me remember where I put my car keys or with some similar problem related to forgetfulness. Wolberg's story puts hypnosis in the category of a mysterious, mystical, miracle cure. *If* hypnosis can aid memory, it would have considerable practical significance. Let's look carefully at the evidence concerning hypnosis and memory.

Wolberg (1982) is a strong believer in recovering buried memories through hypnosis, citing several of his own clinical cases as documentation. For example, he worked with a woman who persistently sleepwalked, locking herself in a closet when she did so. Her husband found her asleep in the closet on the mornings afterward. The woman could not explain her behavior. Under hypnosis she was able to remember that as a child she locked herself in closets when she was angry with her mother so that her mother would have to search for her. She was apparently engaging in the behavior as an adult whenever she was mad at her husband. In other cases that Wolberg mentioned, he used hypnosis to recover pertinent memories and then employed counseling to remedy the problem.

Law Enforcement and Hypnosis

Much of the belief in hypnosis being a memory aid comes from law enforcement work. Arons, a pioneer in teaching hypnosis techniques to police investigators, provided many accounts of hypnosis being used to help in police investigations (1967). The stories ranged from rather mundane episodes such as a 12-year-old boy being helped to remember the last two numbers of a license plate of a getaway car to more dramatic events such as an adult male with total amnesia being able to remember his life history through hypnosis. Arons even included an account of a murderer giving a confession after hypnosis. Law enforcement officials, although reluctant at first, increasingly accepted hypnosis as an aid to enhancing the memory of witnesses. Smith (1983) recounted the use of hypnosis by police in Los Angeles and New York, the FBI, Israeli police, and police in British Columbia. A spokesperson for the Los Angeles police department explained the use of hypnosis in the following manner:

> Frequently when someone is shot, raped, beaten or otherwise attacked, he or she performs a defensive maneuver. They throw up a guard against fright, anxiety, and other traumas. Acting on a survival instinct, they hide the hurt. Through hypnosis, we make the conscious mind passive and communicate with the subconscious to release what's buried there. (Loftus, 1980, pp. 56–57)

As Smith (1983) pointed out, this approach to memory retrieval certainly seems valid based on the many anecdotal reports about hypnosis and crime we have seen on television, in movies, and in popular news magazines.

Therapy and Hypnosis

Therapists use hypnosis to uncover the details of traumatic events for both therapeutic and legal reasons. Gardner and

Olness (1981) summarized a clinical case study of a 17-year-old girl who suffered from amnesia after being raped repeatedly. After hypnosis, she was able to recall the entire event. Later, in therapy, she was able to work through her feelings about the event.

Age regression is a variation of memory recall through hypnosis. In age regression, the person hypnotized supposedly returns to an earlier age rather than merely recalling an event that occurred at an earlier age (Hilgard, 1977). People who undergo age regression typically talk and act in a manner that is consistent with the age to which they have been regressed (Nash, 1987). Wolberg (1982) related a case in which an epileptic was regressed to an age before his first epileptic seizure—an EEG recording made showed no evidence of abnormal brain waves. When the patient was regressed to an age after his first seizure, the EEG showed the epileptic brain wave pattern. Some hypnotists believe that they can regress people to birth, the womb, or even to earlier lives (Hilgard, 1977).

It is clear that many people believe strongly in the ability of hypnosis to aid in the retrieval of memories. According to Orne and Dinges (1989), "the use of hypnosis to block or unblock memory processes has a long and controversial tradition, but continues to be a common feature of the clinical application of hypnosis" (p. 1505). Controversial? Where does the controversy lie?

Smith (1983) attempted to make sense of the controversy surrounding the use of hypnotic recall in legal settings by comparing and contrasting the anecdotal legal accounts of hypnosis with laboratory investigations of hypnosis. Two major differences exist between anecdotal and experimental accounts of hypnosis-aided memory. First, objective verification of the facts is often impossible in anecdotal accounts of memory recall through hypnosis. Although there are accounts of hypnotic recall of license plate numbers of cars involved in crimes, many such "memories" turn out to be incorrect. It is difficult, if not impossible, to verify some memories produced through age regression, particularly if regression takes the person back many years. The second difference between anecdotal and experimental accounts of hypnotic recall is that anecdotal settings do not provide for a control group. We are forced to assume that the recall produced is actually a product of hypnosis and that the recall would not have occurred spontaneously otherwise. Smith pointed out that there are many other variables in a hypnosis setting that might aid memory—a relaxed atmosphere or longer and more detailed questioning, for example. Also, because only some people respond positively to hypnosis, perhaps something about these people makes their recall better under such situations. Let's look at some representative research dealing with hypnosis and memory.

Laboratory Research on Hypnosis

Cooper and London (1973) had participants read a short factual article and take a short-answer test over the article two weeks later. The participants attempted recall twice, once while awake and once while hypnotized, with half recalling first while awake and half recalling first while hypnotized. Cooper and London found no evidence that hypnotized participants recalled any more information than the nonhypnotized participants (both recalled about nine items from the article). However, participants did recall more on the second test than the first (9.2 vs. 8.5 items). Smith (1983) noted that, in the real world, a crime witness typically gives a normal recall account first, followed by a hypnotized recall account. Thus, the apparent heightened recall during hypnosis could actually be a simple order effect of the two recall accounts.

Dhanens and Lundy (1975) had people read a short biography and learn a list of 13 nonsense words. A week later participants tried to recall the information in a normal waking state and made a second recall attempt with or without hypnosis. Some nonhypnotized participants were able to recall as much as some hypnotized participants.

Although these laboratory studies do not support the alleged superiority of hypnotic recall, it is clear that they are different from crime situations. Smith (1983) noted that these differences could create more favorable conditions for hypnotic recall of a crime. Thus, researchers have attempted to use laboratory scrutiny of hypnotic recall in more lifelike settings.

Putnam (1979) selected a group of highly hypnotizable participants and had them watch a videotaped accident between a car and a bicycle. Half the participants were hypnotized during questioning about the accident. Putnam found no differences in recall between hypnotized and nonhypnotized people. Smith (1983) cited similar results showing no advantage for hypnotic recall of a simulated crime in a classroom and of a videotaped bank robbery used to train bank tellers. Thus, more realistic crimelike conditions do not appear to produce any benefit for recall under hypnosis.

In addition to finding no advantage for hypnotic recall, some studies have uncovered a significant disadvantage of using hypnosis to aid recall. In Putnam's (1979) study, the questioning about the car and bicycle accident included six leading questions—questions designed to suggest an incorrect detail or event. Hypnotized participants made more errors on the leading questions than the nonhypnotized participants but were just as confident about their answers. Similar findings occurred in the experiment involving the videotaped bank robbery (Smith, 1983).

In a review of hypnosis effects, Kihlstrom (1985) concluded that "given these findings, it seems difficult to maintain the position that hypnosis yields meaningful increases in memory" (p. 395). Orne and Dinges (1989) added that hypnosis "does increase the person's willingness to report previously uncertain memories with strong conviction" (p. 1516). This result is unfortunate because strong conviction about testimony makes that testimony more believable (Wells et al., 2000). Orne and Dinges (1989) also concluded that people who are hypnotized have "a pronounced tendency to confabulate in those areas where there is little or no recollection; to distort memory to become more congruent with beliefs, hopes, and fantasies; and to incorporate cues from leading questions as factual memories" (p. 1516).

Much the same type of negative conclusion has been reached about hypnotic age regression. For example, Orne (1951) hypnotized nine highly hypnotizable college students and regressed them to age six (the day after their birthday party). The students took the Rorschach ink blot test, drew some pictures, and wrote their name and some words. Several days later they performed the same tasks (unhypnotized) while pretending to be 6 years old. The Rorschach results did not show any consistent patterns of childlike responses when comparing the results with and without hypnosis. Although the pictures and writing looked like those of children, there were inconsistencies that showed through. The drawings were a mix of immature and mature features, and the drawings while hypnotized actually appeared more mature than those made while imagining. The lettering appeared immature but was sometimes too sophisticated for 6-year-olds. For example, one student wrote (with no spelling errors): "I am conducting an experiment which will assess my psychological capacities" (Orne, 1951, p. 219). Orne explained the behavioral changes that were observed as due to "role taking" and not to hypnotic age regression.

Kihlstrom's (1985) review noted that both positive and negative findings are common in age regression studies. Nash (1987) reviewed 80 hypnotic age regression studies and concluded that "there is no evidence for the idea that hypnosis enables subjects to accurately reexperience the events of childhood or to return to developmentally previous modes of functioning" (p. 49). Nash further found that 83% of one-participant studies showed evidence favoring hypnotic age regression but that only 16% of multiple-participant studies that were well designed arrived at the same conclusion. Orne and Dinges (1989) maintained that "careful research has failed to substantiate the belief that accurate memories are reinstated by hypnotic age regression" (p. 1515).

Critical Thinking Errors

Many of the guidelines for critical thinking are not used when dealing with hypnosis. Let's look at two of the prominent ones. Guideline 3 (maintaining an air of skepticism) is often ignored—supporters of hypnosis seem ready to believe that it can accomplish almost anything. Remember: If something seems too good to be true, it usually is. Also, Guideline 7 (examining available evidence) seems to be ignored in two ways. Not only do hypnosis supporters not look for contrary evidence, they ignore the fact that their "evidence" is not experimental in nature.

Thinking about Preconceptions

Why are people so ready to believe that hypnosis aids memory? They have probably seen a news report that reported on a sensational case and accepted it at face value. When we don't check out the facts, we are not thinking critically. Did you know that some states do not allow legal testimony based on hypnosis? In those states hypnosis constitutes tampering with the memory of a witness (Scheflin & Shapiro, 1989). Also, although many professional organizations such as the American Medical Association, American Psychological Association, American

Psychiatric Association, and British Medical Association have approved hypnosis as a *therapeutic* technique, none of them has endorsed it to help the memory of witnesses or crime victims (Orne & Dinges, 1989). In fact, the American Medical Association in 1984 adopted a formal resolution against using hypnosis in this manner.

A problem with our preconceptions concerning hypnotic recall is that much of the favorable evidence comes from anecdotal accounts, law enforcement reports, and case studies. These types of evidence are problematic for drawing conclusions because they are somewhat subjective. Subjectivity sometimes allows us to "find" exactly what we are looking for. Such evidence also makes generalization difficult because only one subject is typically involved. Finally, as Smith (1983) noted, there is no chance for objective verification or a control group in these three methods of data gathering. All these problems do not rule out the possibility that hypnosis aids memory, but they do make it impossible to definitively conclude that hypnosis *causes* any measured increase in memory.

Conclusion

The bottom line on hypnotic recall is not clear at this point. The fact that it is difficult to draw a conclusion illustrates the importance of Guideline 1, the critical thinking skill of examining all sides of an issue and remaining flexible. If we relied simply on our preconceptions, we probably would have no question that hypnosis aids recall. By also examining the empirical evidence, we discover that our preconceived notions may be wrong. Remember in the future to get all sides of the story before making a decision.

Critical Thinking Challenges

1. *Before* you read this chapter, what were your preconceived notions about hypnosis and its effects? How did you form these ideas? Why do you think that people are so willing to accept almost any information about hypnosis?
2. The use of hypnosis to aid recall from memory is based on the assumption that everything is permanently recorded in our memory. Why is this assumption necessary? What im-

plications are there for hypnotic recall if research shows this assumption to be incorrect? In particular, how might the conclusions of this chapter change if the assumption is not true?

3. Try to think of your sixth birthday. Write down as many details of that day as you can. Fold the paper and put it in a safe place. Tomorrow, do the same thing (without referring to your paper from today). The next day, repeat this exercise, concentrating very hard on recalling as much as you possibly can. Now, compare the three sheets of recalled information. Did you recall more on the second and third days than on the first? Is some information on the three sheets inconsistent? How would you explain the differences, whether they are additions, omissions, or inconsistencies? What implications does this exercise have for the typical case studies involving hypnotic recall?

4. Imagine that you are a lawyer in a case in which the star witness's testimony was obtained through hypnosis.
   a. As the defense lawyer, write a one-page essay in which you attempt to have the judge dismiss the case.
   b. As the prosecution lawyer, write a one-page essay in which you attempt to have the judge let the case be tried.

5. Suppose you have a friend who comes to you and confides that she has a feeling in the "back of her mind" that she was sexually abused as a child. She tells you that she wants to try hypnosis to find out whether this is true. How would you respond to her?

References

Arons, H. (1967). *Hypnosis in criminal investigation*. Springfield, IL: Charles C Thomas.

Cooper, L. M., & London, P. (1973). Reactivation of memory by hypnosis and suggestion. *International Journal of Clinical and Experimental Hypnosis, 21,* 312–323.

Dhanens, T. P., & Lundy, R. M. (1975). Hypnotic and waking suggestions and recall. *International Journal of Clinical and Experimental Hypnosis, 23,* 68–79.

Gardner, G. G., & Olness, K. (1981). *Hypnosis and hypnotherapy with children*. New York: Grune & Stratton.

Hilgard, E. R. (1977). *Divided consciousness: Multiple controls in human thought and action*. New York: Wiley.

Kihlstrom, J. F. (1985). Hypnosis. *Annual Review of Psychology, 36,* 385–418.

Loftus, E. (1980). *Memory: Surprising new insights into how we remember and why we forget.* Reading, MA: Addison-Wesley.

Nash, M. (1987). What, if anything, is regressed about hypnotic age regression? A review of the empirical literature. *Psychological Bulletin, 102,* 42–52.

Orne, M. T. (1951). The mechanisms of hypnotic age regression: An experimental study. *Journal of Abnormal and Social Psychology, 46,* 213–225.

Orne, M. T., & Dinges, D. F. (1989). Hypnosis. In H. I. Kaplan & B. J. Sadock (Eds.), *Comprehensive textbook of psychiatry/V* (Vol. 2, pp. 1501–1516). Baltimore: Williams & Wilkins.

Putnam, W. H. (1979). Hypnosis and distortions in eyewitness memory. *International Journal of Clinical and Experimental Hypnosis, 27,* 437–448.

Scheflin, A. W., & Shapiro, J. L. (1989). *Trance on trial.* New York: Guilford.

Smith, M. C. (1983). Hypnotic memory enhancement of witnesses: Does it work? *Psychological Bulletin, 94,* 387–407.

Wells, G. L., Malpass, R. S., Lindsay, R. C. L., Fisher, R. P., Turtle, J. W., & Fulero, S. M. (2000). From the lab to the police station: A successful application of eyewitness research. *American Psychologist, 55,* 581–598.

Wolberg, L. R. (1982). *Hypnosis: Is it for you?* New York: Dembner Books.

7

🔥

Conditioning and Advertising

Why do we buy the products that we buy? Why do we like the brands that we like? Why buy a brand X car rather than a brand Y car? After we have established our preferences, why are we willing to replace products that we like and that work with new and untried products? These questions dealing with consumer behavior have complex answers. Giving complete answers to such questions is beyond the scope of this book. However, in this chapter, we will look at one part of the answer that you may not have considered previously.

When we think about these questions, most of us probably respond with a preconceived answer something like "I compare the price, quality, and features of the various products and then make a choice among the alternatives." This type of response, of course, portrays us as intelligent, rational, thinking consumers. It is precisely the type of answer we would give if queried about our choices in a political election.

Is there, however, something much more elemental about our purchasing choices, even our voting choices? Do we, perhaps, rely on intuition or hunches when we make choices? Is it possible that these intuitions are not even of our own making? Evidence exists that we may form some product preferences through the mechanism of classical conditioning. Let's briefly review classical conditioning.

Classical Conditioning

You probably remember classical conditioning as involving a dog salivating to a bell or some similar stimulus. How could a slobbering dog have anything to do with our consumer behavior?

Let's remember what happened when the dog was conditioned to salivate in response to the bell. A neutral stimulus, the bell (the conditioned stimulus, or CS), was repeatedly paired with another stimulus, the meat powder (the unconditioned stimulus, or UCS), that automatically caused a response, salivation (the unconditioned response, or UCR). After many pairings of these stimuli, the bell gradually came to cause the response (salivation, now the conditioned response, or CR). Thus, the bell had gained meaning through repeated pairings with a meaningful stimulus.

You probably also recall that classical conditioning can be used to elicit emotional responses. Do you remember Watson's experiment with little Albert? Watson repeatedly paired a loud noise (UCS) and a white rat (CS). Albert originally liked the rat but came to fear it (CR) because the noise naturally caused fear (UCR) and Albert came to associate that noise with the rat. If advertisers could classically condition positive emotions with their products, would we like the products more (and potentially buy more of the product)? Let's look at the evidence.

Conditioning and Evaluation: Positive Findings

Smith and Engel (1968) devised a printed automobile advertisement for participants to study and then rate the advertised car. Half the participants, both males and females, saw an ad that had a female model standing beside the car; the other half saw the same ad without the model. The model was simply standing beside the car, not interacting with it in any manner. The picture of the model came from *Playboy* magazine; she was clad in black lace panties and a sleeveless sweater. Participants who saw the ad with the model rated the car as more appealing, lively, youthful, and better designed. These people also believed that the car was more expensive, faster, less safe, and more powerful. Smith and Engel asked some of the participants whether they thought the model had influenced their judgments. As you might predict based on your own preconceptions, they denied that the model had swayed them. Participants made comments such as: "I don't let anything but the thing itself influence my judgments. The other is just propaganda." "I never let myself be blinded by advertising; the car itself is what counts" (Smith & Engel, 1968, p. 681). Although no specific mention of conditioning was made, it is likely that participants associated the model and the car in making their ratings.

Gorn (1982) appears to be the first researcher to directly test the effects of classical conditioning on product preference. Gorn told participants that they were listening to music used to advertise pens; an advertising agency had chosen the music. He used two pretested musical selections—one liked and one disliked in pretesting—and two neutral colors of pens, light blue and beige. Each person participated in one of four groups: blue or beige pen paired with liked or disliked music. After viewing a slide of the pen while listening to music, each person evaluated the music. Upon leaving, they were free to choose either a blue or beige pen for their participation. Gorn found that the type of music strongly influenced pen selection: 79% of the participants chose the pen color they saw when it was paired with the liked music; only 30% chose the pen color they saw when it was paired with the disliked music. Gorn concluded that the musical selection was associated, through conditioning, with a particular pen color. When the music was liked, participants tended to choose the pen that they saw. However, when the music was disliked, they were more likely to choose the pen they had *not* seen.

Gorn's experiment triggered much research investigating the effects of classical conditioning in advertising and consumer situations. For example, Bierley, McSweeney, and Vannieuwkerk (1985) found that geometric figures paired with music from *Star Wars* received high preference ratings. Stuart, Shimp, and Engle (1987) showed that pairing "brand L" toothpaste with pleasant landscape scenes raised the evaluation of the toothpaste.

Conditioning and Evaluation: Negative Findings

Despite the successful research mentioned previously, some studies dealing with classical conditioning and evaluation of products have yielded mixed findings. Gresham and Shimp (1985) attempted conditioning of ten different brands with liked and disliked advertisements. Only three of the ten brands showed evidence of the expected conditioning. Blair and Shimp (1992) were able to condition a negative attitude toward a fictitious brand of shirts by pairing the brand with disliked music, but they were unable to condition a positive attitude with liked music.

Some research on classical conditioning and evaluation has yielded decidedly negative findings. Allen and Madden

(1985) attempted to replicate Gorn's (1982) experiment by asso-
ciating different pen colors with pleasant and unpleasant humor
rather than music. The choice of pen color was unaffected by
the humor. Kellaris and Cox (1989) attempted a more exact replication of Gorn's experiment by pairing liked and disliked music with different pen colors. They found no evidence that participants' pen selection was influenced by the music they heard.

Making Sense of Disparate Findings

After reviewing the evidence, we are faced with contradictory
findings. In such a situation, avoiding preconceived notions and
using critical thinking are of paramount importance. Preconceived notions often derail our search for correct answers. Because we carry such notions with us, we may choose to believe
the first piece of evidence we find that supports our ideas. Such
behavior, of course, does not exemplify critical thinking.

When we are faced with disparate findings, critical thinking offers several possible avenues for inquiry. One approach,
of course, is to evaluate the research findings that do not agree
to determine whether some of the studies are flawed. If flaws
exist, the findings of those studies are questionable; there may
be no controversy after we discount the flawed results. A second
approach is to conclude that the various findings seem sound,
which leaves the controversy intact. In such a case, critical thinkers typically search for a new explanation—an idea or theory
that can combine and reconcile the disparate findings. A third
approach mirrors the second approach, except that a reconciling idea cannot be found. In this instance, a critical thinker must
decide that it is simply impossible to draw a conclusion at the
present time.

What tack should we take with the findings regarding classical conditioning and evaluation? There are no obvious flaws in
the various studies cited in this chapter, so we should examine
other literature in order to determine whether we can find a uni-
fying principle or theory to explain these findings. Gorn (1982)
conducted a second experiment that is rarely cited in the literature (his first experiment supporting classical conditioning of
pen choice draws the most attention). In this second experiment, participants viewed one pen paired with liked music and
a second pen paired with important information about the pen.
They were asked to evaluate the effectiveness of these market-

ing approaches. Half the participants were told *before* seeing the ads that they would be allowed to choose a pack of pens after the experiment; the remaining people were not told about the free pens until after the experiment. As Gorn predicted, participants who were preinformed showed a strong preference (71%) for the pen advertised with information whereas the later-informed group preferred (63%) the pen advertised with music. Gorn believed that putting people into a decision-making mode ahead of time heightened their attention to the information contained in the commercial. On the other hand, Gorn said that people who did not think about a choice ahead of time were susceptible to the conditioning manipulation.

Petty and Cacioppo (1986) conceptualized such results in their elaboration likelihood model of attitude change. They referred to two routes for attitude change: a central route, used when people are involved with an issue and are willing to think about it, and a peripheral route, used when people are not highly involved with an issue. According to Petty and Cacioppo, the peripheral route can employ factors that are irrelevant to a message, such as the attractiveness or prestige of the communicator, how pleasant the surroundings are, and so on. Thus, the model predicts that people who are critical buyers will be swayed by information but not hype, whereas casual or unthinking buyers will be more impressed by flash than substance. Petty, Cacioppo, and Schumann (1983) composed fictitious razor ads for participants to read. They manipulated involvement with the ad by telling some participants the razors would be marketed in their area soon and by promising them free razors. In addition, the razor ads varied in their informativeness and in whether they used celebrity endorsers. The results showed that high-involvement participants (those who would have a chance to buy the razors) were influenced most by the informative ads (central route) whereas low-involvement participants (those who would not be able to buy the razors) were more influenced by ads using celebrities (peripheral route).

Bruner (1990) reviewed 16 marketing-related studies that used music as a potential influencing agent. He concluded that "music is likely to have its greatest effect when consumers have high affective and/or low cognitive involvement with the product. Product categories fitting this description for most consumers include jewelry, sportswear, cosmetics, and beer" (p. 101). He pointed out that consumers with high cognitive involvement—such as those buying cars, computers, and insurance—

would be less affected by music. Bruner's conclusions clearly fit the elaboration likelihood model.

It seems that the elaboration likelihood model can explain the classical conditioning and evaluation data summarized in this chapter. If potential consumers are relatively uninvolved or disinterested in a purchasing decision, then classical conditioning can have the power to affect that decision. If advertisers can create some type of positive feeling about a product through classical conditioning, that positive feeling might pay off with higher sales down the line.

Critical Thinking Errors

When we insist that we make our purchases through reasoned and rational thinking, we are ignoring Guideline 3 (maintaining an air of skepticism). It is much more difficult to think critically about our behavior than about other people's behavior, but we must apply our skeptical attitude to ourselves also—we must follow Guideline 1 (tolerate ambiguity and uncertainty) and keep an open mind.

Thinking about Preconceptions

Most of us probably overestimate our use of reason and rationality in making decisions, part of a tendency we have to see ourselves in a favorable light—the self-serving bias (Myers, 1999). We would be slow to admit that any advertising could ever influence our purchases. Yet the data in this chapter imply that we can be influenced by a process as simple as classical conditioning.

An interesting point about influence through classical conditioning is that the process can be quite subtle. Advertisers do not have to scream "buy our product!" Instead, they can settle for creating within you a pleasant mood so that you will reexperience that mood when you see their product at the store. Without thinking (low involvement), you may purchase that particular brand. You can later rationalize your decision by describing how good the product is, thus seeming to show high involvement. Subtlety is the key to classical conditioning and evaluation—watch out for it!

Conclusion

Can you resist the power of classical conditioning in evaluation? Sure! Do you *want* to resist its power? Maybe . . . maybe not.

The elaboration likelihood model implies that you can resist the subtle influence of classical conditioning by being highly involved or interested in an issue. However, is it really worth the trouble of being highly involved in each and every purchasing decision that you make? If you're buying a car, you should certainly look past that attractive model posing with the car. Buying a car is a major decision, with many long-lasting ramifications. In contrast, buying a particular brand of toothpaste or soap or laundry detergent is probably not a life-changing decision (despite what the commercials imply!). You probably don't have the cognitive energy to become deeply involved in every consumer decision you make. Thus, you are easy prey for classical conditioning of peripheral factors to affect your less important decisions. If this bothers you, keep your guard up—watch for conditioning attempts in advertising. Otherwise, you can simply be aware of the effects of classical conditioning and continue to pay a few pennies more for some products because their clever commercials have conditioned you to like those brands. It's just not that big a deal in some instances!

Critical Thinking Challenges

1. Watch about 20 commercials. Choose the one that, to you, best exemplifies the use of classical conditioning of evaluation and describe it. What are the UCS, UCR, CS, and CR? How does this commercial use classical conditioning so effectively?
2. Repeat Exercise 1 with a print advertisement from a newspaper or magazine.
3. In comparing the two types of presentation in Exercises 1 and 2 (video versus print), which seems more effective in establishing conditioning of evaluation? Why?
4. Using the elaboration likelihood model, what should an advertising campaign for a 35mm camera emphasize? What about a campaign for a new snack food? Explain your rationale for each set of features.
5. In the introduction to this chapter, voting choices were mentioned as a decision that might be affected by classical

conditioning. Given the information in this chapter, develop a scenario in which this possibility occurs. Also, develop a scenario in which classical conditioning would *not* affect voting choice.

References

Allen, C. T., & Madden, T. J. (1985). A closer look at classical conditioning. *Journal of Consumer Research, 12,* 301–315.

Bierley, C., McSweeney, F. K., & Vannieuwkerk, R. (1985). Classical conditioning of preferences for stimuli. *Journal of Consumer Research, 12,* 316–323.

Blair, M. E., & Shimp, T. A. (1992). Consequences of an unpleasant experience with music: A second-order negative conditioning perspective. *Journal of Advertising, 21,* 35–43.

Bruner, G. C., III. (1990). Music, mood, and marketing. *Journal of Marketing, 54*(4), 94–104.

Gorn, G. J. (1982). The effects of music in advertising on choice behavior: A classical conditioning approach. *Journal of Marketing, 46,* 94–101.

Gresham, L. G., & Shimp, T. A. (1985). Attitude toward the advertisement and brand attitudes: A classical conditioning perspective. *Journal of Advertising, 14,* 10–17, 49.

Kellaris, J. J., & Cox, A. D. (1989). The effects of background music in advertising: A reassessment. *Journal of Consumer Research, 16,* 113–118.

Myers, D. G. (1999). *Social psychology* (6th ed.). New York: McGraw-Hill.

Petty, R. E., & Cacioppo, J. T. (1986). *Communication and persuasion: Central and peripheral routes to attitude change.* New York: Springer-Verlag.

Petty, R. E., Cacioppo, J. T., & Schumann, D. (1983). Central and peripheral routes to advertising effectiveness: The moderating role of involvement. *Journal of Consumer Research, 10,* 135–146.

Smith, G. H., & Engel, R. (1968). Influence of a female model on perceived characteristics of an automobile. *Proceedings of the American Psychological Association, 3,* 681–682.

Stuart, E. W., Shimp, T. A., & Engle, R. W. (1987). Classical conditioning of consumer attitudes: Four experiments in an advertising context. *Journal of Consumer Research, 14,* 334–349.

8

🔥

Biases in Memory

If you are like most people, you long ago gave up the idea that your memory is infallible. You have become accustomed to the occasional memory lapse—not being able to remember someone's name, forgetting where you put your car keys, or failing to recall a specific term on an exam. However, you probably continue to have a high degree of confidence in the accuracy of the memories that you do retrieve. We like to think of our memories as sophisticated copy machines or tape recorders. When we recall something, we are usually certain it is correct— or is it? In this chapter we will examine some common biases in our memory. These biases can make our recall less accurate than we believe it to be.

Prior Knowledge

Information that we have already stored in memory can affect the accuracy of information that we process subsequently. In such cases, we allow our preconceptions to influence our memory.

In a classic study, Bartlett (1932) had participants read an American Indian folktale and recall it after various intervals of time. Bartlett found that participants' recall depended on what they already knew. They distorted or left out details of Indian folklore that were unfamiliar. Elements that fit their stereotypes of Indians were added to the story.

Snyder and Uranowitz (1978) also demonstrated the effect of stereotypes on memory. Participants read the life history of a fictitious woman (Betty) including the fact that she occasionally dated men. *After* reading her history, some participants learned that Betty was a lesbian and some heard that she was heterosexual. What happened to the participants' memories? People who thought Betty was a lesbian were more likely to "remember" that Betty never dated men than those people who thought Betty was heterosexual. Thus, preconceptions, in the form of stereotypes, can bias our memory.

Belief Perseverance

We often form an opinion about something and later find out that the information we based our opinion on was incorrect. The logical thing to do in such an instance is to change our biased opinion—but do we?

Anderson, Lepper, and Ross (1980) had people read descriptions of firefighters who performed well either because they were risk-takers or because they were cautious. Participants were then asked to develop reasons why the particular trait their firefighters exhibited (risk-taking or caution) made them good firefighters. Afterward, participants learned that the experimenters had fabricated the relationship between risk-taking and firefighter performance and that the true relationship was unknown. When asked to speculate about the true relationship based on their personal beliefs and *not* the fictitious information, participants showed a strong tendency to reason in a manner consistent with the fictitious information they had read previously.

Lepper, Ross, and Lau (1986) found that incorrect information about one's ability that is later discounted can continue to affect one's self-perception. They had participants try to solve puzzles after instruction from a teacher. Afterward, some people found out that their success or failure was actually due to the quality of instruction rather than to their own ability and effort. Nonetheless, regardless of the quality of instruction they received, participants who were successful thought they would be more successful at similar tasks in the future, and participants who were unsuccessful thought they would do poorly at similar tasks. These differences in self-perception persisted several weeks later on more general measures of academic ability and preference. Thus, students lowered their self-evaluations even when they had good reasons to explain away their failures. This memory bias could be quite harmful in the classroom!

Leading Questions

You have probably seen courtroom dramas in which an attorney objects to a question because it is a leading question—one that attempts to lead the witness to say something that the other attorney wants to hear. Can leading questions actually have an effect on memory?

Loftus and Palmer (1974) showed participants films of car accidents and then asked questions about the films. Loftus asked some participants "About how fast were the cars going when they *hit* each other?" Others were asked "About how fast were the cars going when they *smashed into* each other?" Participants who were asked about the cars *hitting* each other gave estimates of 34 miles per hour whereas those asked about the cars *smashing* estimated the speed as almost 41 miles per hour. In a second experiment, Loftus and Palmer showed a film of an accident and used the same two questions about speed. A week later participants returned and answered more questions about the accident, including "Did you see any broken glass?" (there was no broken glass in the film). The leading question appeared to further affect participants' memories as 32% of those who were asked the "smashed" question remembered seeing broken glass compared to only 14% of those asked the "hit" question.

Leading questions can also affect visual recognition memory, which is normally highly accurate. Loftus, Miller, and Burns (1978) showed two groups of participants a series of slides that depicted a sports car traveling through an intersection and hitting a pedestrian. The groups saw identical slides except that one group saw the car pass a yield sign at the intersection and the other group saw a stop sign. After seeing the slides, participants answered questions about the slides. Half of each group answered a question that was consistent with the intersection's sign (for example, they saw a yield sign and were asked about a yield sign), and half answered an inconsistent question (for example, they saw a stop sign and were asked about a yield sign). Participants later took a visual recognition test by seeing pairs of slides and choosing the one they had seen before. The critical test involved the two intersection slides. Participants who answered a consistent question recognized the correct intersection slide 75% of the time whereas those who answered an inconsistent question were correct only 41% of the time. Clearly, leading questions do seem to alter our memories.

Encoding and Retrieval Perspectives

Because people have different motivations, desires, and previous experiences, we have different perspectives when we store or recall information. It is possible that these different perspectives can influence or bias our memories. You can probably remember reminiscing about an experience you shared with a friend. As you dredged up old memories, you may have been surprised to find out that the two of you remember slightly different accounts of the event. You may have had a similar experience after being involved in a traffic accident. Your account of the accident may be somewhat different from what people in the other car remember. These differences probably do not represent attempts to distort the truth, but simple differences in perspective.

Anderson and Pichert (1978) had participants read a story about a house from one of two perspectives, a homebuyer or a burglar. After a short delay, participants recalled as many details about the house as they could. People who read the passage from a burglar's perspective recalled more details about the house that would be relevant to a burglar (for example, valuable coin collection, unlocked door, tall hedges hiding the house) rather than to a homebuyer. Those who read as homebuyers recalled more details relevant to that perspective (for example, leaking roof, damp and musty basement, fresh paint). This effect of perspective was stronger for the burglar perspective. In explaining this effect, Anderson and Pichert noted that college students probably have more experience with the perspective of burglars (from television and movies) than of homebuyers.

After the participants' initial recall attempt, Anderson and Pichert added an interesting twist. They asked people to make a second recall attempt from the different perspective (burglar to homebuyer and vice versa). Participants recalled 10% more of the information relevant to their new perspective and 21% less of the information that was now irrelevant on the second recall attempt. This difference had to occur due to the retrieval perspective because all the information had already been encoded. Thus, it is clear that not only can a particular perspective bias memory, but reversing that perspective can result in a reversal of that bias.

Stress and Anxiety

We experience stress and anxiety on a regular basis in our daily lives. Is it possible that these experiences affect our memory? Researchers have studied anxiety from both state and trait perspectives. State anxiety is related to a specific event or situation, such as making a speech before a large audience. Trait anxiety is related to the individual, as some people generally experience higher levels of anxiety than normal. We can look at the effects of stress and anxiety on memory in both state and trait situations.

A good example of stress and anxiety affecting memory in a statelike situation is found in eyewitness testimony. Deffenbacher (1983) noted that "weapon focus" often causes poor memory for crimes. If a criminal uses a weapon during the offense, victims tend to focus their attention on the weapon rather than on the criminal. Of course, it is not ethical to expose experimental subjects to stressors such as those that might occur in actual crimes, so researchers have had to improvise in the lab. For example, Loftus and Burns (1982) showed participants a series of slides depicting a bank robbery. Toward the end of the slides, half the participants saw a bystander shot. People who saw the shooting showed poorer memory for a specific detail in the slides than people who saw no shooting. This effect occurred for both recall (4.3% vs. 27.9% correct) and recognition (28% correct vs. 52% correct). In related research, Kramer and colleagues (1991) showed participants a series of travel scenes. Half the people saw a traumatic autopsy slide in the middle of the scenes. People who saw the stressful slide showed reduced memory for the scenes following the autopsy slide (32% correct recall) compared to participants who did not see a stressful slide (52% correct recall).

Siegel and Loftus (1978) examined the effects of traitlike anxiety and stress on memory. They had participants complete a variety of questionnaires designed to measure anxiety, self-preoccupation, and life stress. These participants saw a series of slides that depicted a purse-snatching episode and later answered 30 questions concerning the incident. Siegel and Loftus found that participants who were more anxious and preoccupied performed more poorly on the eyewitness test. Along the same lines, Zanni and Offermann (1978) found that people who scored high in neuroticism (level of arousal) were more likely to make errors in recalling details from a film.

Some studies have actually shown heightened recall under stressful conditions. In his review of the literature, Deffenbacher (1983) concluded that these studies tended to manipulate only low levels of arousal. Studies that created arousal more appropriate to actual crime conditions found that stress debilitated memory. Thus, it seems that strong stress or anxiety, whether temporary or more permanent, can impair memory.

Critical Thinking Errors

When we hold onto our preconception that memory is completely accurate or that it is an exact copy of what we have witnessed, we are violating Guideline 5 (avoiding oversimplification). Memory is simply too complex for us to engage in such simplified thinking. Thus, to set ourselves right, we must use Guideline 4 (separating fact from opinion) and Guideline 7 (examining available evidence). When we engage in these two processes, we find that memory is not infallible and is subject to various biases.

Thinking about Preconceptions

It appears unrealistic to think of our memories as exact recordings of the events and stimuli that we encounter. We saw, for example, that stereotypes or stress and anxiety affect memories as we store them. It also appears that retrieving a memory as it was originally stored is not a certainty. Leading questions and different perspectives appear to alter our memories even as we retrieve them from storage. Thus, it appears that we should abandon our preconceived notion of memory as an infallible event recorder. Our memories are subject to distortion from a variety of sources—a fact that we should be careful to remember.

Conclusion

This chapter emphasizes the malleable nature of memory—the notion that memory is an active process. This label simply means that memories can change as we store them, as they are in storage, or as we retrieve them. Viewing memory as a dynamic and changing process rather than as a static process gives us reason to be more impressed by our ability to remember things accurately, something that you probably accept as a given.

Is it possible to avoid these biases and improve the accuracy of your memory? Being aware of some of these memory pitfalls may make it possible to minimize their influence. For example, if you are aware of your stereotypes, perhaps you can recognize occasions when they have influenced your memory. However, some of these factors are impossible to avoid. If you ever witness a bank robbery or violent crime, you cannot avoid the stress and anxiety of that experience, nor can you undo their effects on your memory. You can, however, realize that your memory may be less accurate in such a situation and lower your confidence accordingly.

You also have some ammunition with which you can critically examine the circumstances of people's memories. If you realize that one of these factors has occurred, you can call into question any recall that occurred after the situation. Again, such information should help you be a critical consumer of information based on memory—whether your own or someone else's.

The message for critical thinking appears clear. Maintain a healthy skepticism about the information that you (or others) remember (Guideline 3). Whenever possible, try to use another source to verify information that is recalled.

Critical Thinking Challenges

1. Choose one of the factors affecting memory summarized in this chapter. Suppose you are assigned to tell people how to avoid this particular memory bias. What would you tell them?
2. Think of a time that you fell victim to a biased memory. Describe the situation. What factor(s) helped to distort your memory? Knowing what you know now, what would you do differently if the same situation occurred again?
3. Research shows that eyewitness testimony is a powerful factor in legal cases. Based on information from this chapter, develop three arguments why jurors should be less persuaded by such testimony.
4. Suppose you hear two people recount their memories of the same event after several years have passed. The two accounts differ to some degree. Do you think it is possible that both people are recalling correctly? Why or why not?

References

Anderson, C. A., Lepper, M. R., & Ross, L. (1980). Perseverance of social theories: The role of explanation in the persistence of discredited information. *Journal of Personality and Social Psychology, 39,* 1037–1049.

Anderson, R. C., & Pichert, J. W. (1978). Recall of previously un-recallable information following a shift in perspective. *Journal of Verbal Learning and Verbal Behavior, 17,* 1–12.

Bartlett, F. C. (1932). *Remembering: A study in experimental and social psychology.* Cambridge, England: Cambridge University Press.

Deffenbacher, K. A. (1983). The influence of arousal on reliability of testimony. In S. M. A. Lloyd-Bostock and B. R. Clifford (Eds.), *Evaluating witness evidence: Recent psychological research and new perspectives* (pp. 235–251). Chichester, England: Wiley.

Kramer, T. H., Buckhout, R., Fox, P., Widman, E., & Tusche, B. (1991). Effects of stress on recall. *Applied Cognitive Psychology, 5,* 483–488.

Lepper, M. R., Ross, L., & Lau, R. R. (1986). Persistence of inaccurate beliefs about the self: Perseverance effects in the classroom. *Journal of Personality and Social Psychology, 50,* 482–491.

Loftus, E. F., & Burns, T. E. (1982). Mental shock can produce retrograde amnesia. *Memory & Cognition, 10,* 318–323.

Loftus, E. F., Miller, D. G., & Burns, H. J. (1978). Semantic integration of verbal information into a visual memory. *Journal of Experimental Psychology: Human Learning and Memory, 4,* 19–31.

Loftus, E. F., & Palmer, J. C. (1974). Reconstruction of automobile destruction: An example of the interaction between language and memory. *Journal of Verbal Learning and Verbal Behavior, 13,* 585–589.

Siegel, J. M., & Loftus, E. F. (1978). Impact of anxiety and life stress upon eyewitness testimony. *Bulletin of the Psychonomic Society, 12,* 479–480.

Snyder, M., & Uranowitz, S. W. (1978). Reconstructing the past: Some cognitive consequences of person perception. *Journal of Personality and Social Psychology, 36,* 941–950.

Zanni, G. R., & Offermann, J. T. (1978). Eyewitness testimony: An exploration of question wording upon recall as a function of neuroticism. *Perceptual and Motor Skills, 46,* 163–166.

9

❦

IQ Is Forever—Isn't It?

As a college student today, you are part of the "tested generation." By that phrase, I mean that you have taken standardized tests on a routine basis since you were young. You can probably still remember taking a day or two out of your grade school routine to take that year's achievement tests—learning what a no. 2 pencil is, how to color in the circles completely, to erase thoroughly, and so on. You also may remember that important decisions regarding your schooling and future were made on the basis of such test scores.

This emphasis on standardized testing can be tied to the development of mental ability tests—what we commonly call intelligence tests—in the early part of this century. Because these tests were helpful in categorizing students of different abilities and in predicting school performance, researchers developed many other standardized tests.

There are many critical issues regarding psychological testing. The majority of such issues revolve around intelligence tests. In this chapter, we will examine a common assumption—namely that IQs remain constant over time. This assumption is based on the related assumption that intelligence is a reflection of your mental capacity (Shaffer, 1999). If this assumption is true, it seems that intelligence would be fairly constant—your mental capacity would presumably be set by heredity and should not change over time. Both the assumptions that intelligence is determined solely by heredity and that intelligence tests measure mental capacity have been severely challenged, but the assumption of IQ stability seems to linger, at least in the minds of the general public. Let's look at some research evidence to determine whether IQs remain stable over time.

Infant IQ Tests

Several tests have been developed to measure intelligence in infants and very young children (Kaplan & Saccuzzo, 1997). The best-known and most widely used scale of this type is the *Bayley Scales of Infant Development,* designed for use with children who are 2 to 30 months old (Shaffer, 1999). According to Kaplan and Saccuzzo, "the Bayley is the most psychometrically sound test of its kind" (p. 311). On the Bayley, infants are measured on a motor scale and a mental scale. Scores from these scales are combined to yield a DQ (developmental quotient). Although the resulting score is not termed an IQ, it is used to compare infants to norms derived from age-group peers. As you might guess, researchers have correlated Bayley scores with IQ scores obtained in childhood. With the exception of predicting children who will be retarded, Bayley scores are not useful for predicting childhood IQs (Honzik, 1983; Kaplan & Saccuzzo, 1997). Other infant tests of intelligence show the same pattern—they have "no long-term predictive validity for normal children . . . such tests do have some prognostic value for low-scoring infants" (Lewis & Sullivan, 1985, p. 568).

Childhood IQ Tests

As children grow older, they can be tested with the better-known intelligence scales such as the Stanford-Binet test (beginning at age 2) or the Wechsler Preschool and Primary Scale of Intelligence (beginning at age 4). In a typical study, children will take an intelligence test at two different times. Researchers will then correlate those two sets of scores to determine how similar they are. If children make similar scores each time, the correlation will be high (up to 1.00 if the scores are identical). If there is no correspondence between the scores, the correlation would be nonexistent (a correlation of 0.00). Honzik, Macfarlane, and Allen (1948) found fairly high correlations between IQ scores of children tested at various ages. As you can see in Table 9-1, IQs become more stable as children grow older and as the interval between the tests decreases.

However, the statistics in Table 9-1 may be somewhat misleading. The correlations shown were based on large groups of children (150 to 250 depending on the age tested) and do not necessarily reflect what might happen with any individual child.

Table 9-1
Correlations of Children's IQ Scores

Child's Age at Testing	Correlation with IQ at Age 10	Correlation with IQ at Age 18
2	.37	.31
4	.64	.42
6	.74	.61
8	.88	.70
10	—	.73
12	.87	.77

Source: Data from Honzik, Macfarlane, & Allen, 1948.

For example, Honzik, Macfarlane, and Allen (1948) also found that 58% of the children in their study showed an IQ change of 15 points or more between age 6 and 18. Such a fluctuation would be large enough to relabel a child from "retarded" to "low average" or from "high average" to "gifted." As you can imagine, the differences in these labels would be quite significant. This finding of individual fluctuation is not unusual. McCall, Applebaum, and Hogarty (1973) studied 80 children who regularly took IQ tests (as many as 17 assessments) from age 2½ to 17. They found large IQ variations in over half of the participants, with an average fluctuation of 28.5 points. One of every three children showed a change of more than 30 points and one in seven changed more than 40 points, with a maximum change of 74 IQ points. Hindley and Owen (1978) reported finding similar fluctuations, with 25% of their participants' scores changing at least 10 points between ages 14 and 17.

The results in the previous two paragraphs present a problem for thinking critically about the stability of IQ scores. In the group data, IQs appear to be stable. For the individual scores, however, IQs are potentially quite variable. Let's look further.

Adolescent IQ Tests

By adolescence, IQ scores tend to be more stable. For example, Hindley and Owen (1978) reported correlations between IQs at ages 11 and 14 of .69, at 11 and 17 of .68, and at 14 and 17 of .87. Table 9-1 shows similar correlations between IQs at ages 10 and 18 and also at 12 and 18.

IQs of adolescents can even be used for predicting middle-age IQs with a good degree of accuracy. Bayley (1966) reported results from the Berkeley Growth Study, begun in 1928, that measured participants' intelligence from 1 month to 36 years of age. She found correlations between IQs at ages 16 and 36 to be .97 for males and .69 for females. Bayley noted that the gender difference in correlations is not unusual and was likely due to "the difference in educational and occupational goals of males and females" (1966, p. 135). These people were tested in the 1940s and 1960s; the difference in goals between males and females was probably greater then than today.

Eichorn, Hunt, and Honzik (1981) reported correlations between IQ scores at late adolescence (17 to 18) and middle age (36 to 48) of .83 for males and .77 for females. This gender difference was not significant, but the correlation from adolescence to adulthood remained strong. However, just as with childhood IQ scores, marked individual fluctuations in scores were seen from test to test; about half of the 250 people tested showed increases or decreases of at least 10 IQ points (Eichorn, Mussen, Clausen, Haan, & Honzik, 1981).

Adult IQ Tests

The question about stability of IQ changes slightly when people reach adulthood. No longer are researchers as interested in trying to predict a later IQ score from an earlier IQ score. Instead, they are interested in the question of whether the IQ remains constant across the life span. Studies in the early part of this century indicated that IQ peaked in early adulthood and then began to steadily decline (Sigelman, 1999). However, these studies used the cross-sectional approach, comparing people in different age groups at the same period. Longitudinal studies, comparing the same people over long time periods, showed that people's IQs either remained constant or actually increased from early adulthood to middle age. These studies found only small declines in old age. However, both methodologies have been criticized—cross-sectional studies for failing to hold educational opportunities constant, and longitudinal studies for subjects dropping out (Sigelman, 1991).

Schaie (1983, 1996) developed the sequential approach, which combines cross-sectional and longitudinal approaches, to study the relationship of age and IQ. Schaie found that *when*

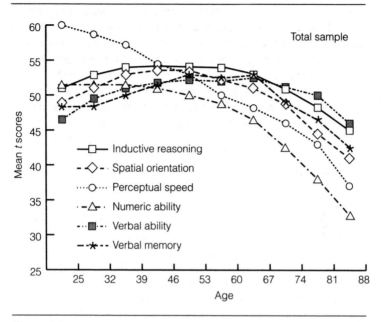

Figure 9-1
Age Changes in Mental Abilities Across the Life Span
From *Intellectual Development in Adulthood: The Seattle Longitudinal Study,* by
K. Warner Schaie, p. 128. Copyright 1996, Cambridge University Press.

one is born is at least as important in determining IQ as is one's
age. Thus, being born later in time gives one the advantages of
better education, health care, and nutrition, all of which are beneficial to IQ. Figure 9-1 shows the relationship Schaie (1996)
found between various intellectual abilities and age. As you can
see, peak performance occurs in middle age for some abilities,
and decline is not serious until much later in life than was originally thought. Schaie (1996) concluded, "It is not until the 80s
are reached that the average older adult will fall below the
middle range of performance for young adults" (p. 353).

Critical Thinking Errors

Merely asking whether IQs are stable over life spans may violate
Guideline 5 (don't oversimplify). The evidence in this chapter
has shown different answers depending on how you ask the
question. If we look at large groups of people to determine

stability, IQs seem to be fairly stable (due to the high correlations), except at very young ages. However, the research also shows that the IQs for any individual may show considerable variability. Thus, our question needs to be more specific to yield a good answer.

As I pointed out in the chapter introduction, the belief in stable IQs is probably related to a belief that IQ is primarily determined by hereditary factors. Thus, the problem may lie with Guideline 2 (identifying inherent biases and assumptions). Broadening your conception of IQ to include environmental determinants also allows the assumption of changeable IQs. By using Guideline 6 (making logical inferences), this change in assumptions opens a new way of interpreting IQ.

Thinking about Preconceptions

If you carry the preconception that, based on IQ scores, people are either "smart for life" or "dumb forever," this chapter should give you some doubts about that idea. It appears, at least for some people, IQ is a fluid trait—it can change considerably over time. This notion of changing IQs seems to be particularly true at younger ages. Considerable evidence exists to support the notion that the younger the person is when his or her IQ is tested, the less confidence we should place in that score.

Conclusion

This chapter illustrates one of the pitfalls of the testing movement—that of placing too much emphasis on a single score. Let's look at a potential peril of using IQ scores without other information: the notion of expectancies.

Many of you reading this book will probably remember a parent going to school for a conference about your aptitude test scores. You may have heard that you were not working up to your potential. Although hearing this information was probably not a pleasant experience, you were the lucky kids. What happens to children who score very low on aptitude tests? They probably get labeled as "lacking potential" or "learning disabled" or something similar. Such labels, in turn, can lead parents, relatives, teachers, and school administrators to have lowered expectations for those children. They may be expected to fail.

Let's examine a classic study about the effects of expectations, which can directly affect behavior and performance. Rosenthal and Jacobson (1968) led teachers to believe, on the basis of aptitude test scores, that a group of children (actually randomly selected) were about to blossom intellectually. At the end of the school year, those children showed a larger increase in IQ scores when compared to children in the control group. Rosenthal's (1991) review of such research has shown that this effect is not universal, but interpersonal expectations do affect performance about 45% of the time in everyday situations (based on 167 studies) and 35% of the time in laboratory experiments (based on 281 studies). Thus, expectations can play an important role in determining behavior and performance, a phenomenon known as the self-fulfilling prophecy.

Finally, let me add a note of irony to the notions of the two previous paragraphs. Despite the fact that test scores can label students and create self-fulfilling expectations, IQ scores are not even the best predictor of students' grades. According to Minton and Schneider (1980), the best predictor of future grades is a student's earlier grades.

It seems clear that we would be wise to reduce the emphasis we place on IQ scores, especially IQ scores obtained early in a child's life or those obtained many years ago. When we deal with factors, such as grades and school, that are important in determining the future of children, it is probably wise to err on the side of caution. As Honzik, Macfarlane, and Allen (1948) wrote, "The observed fluctuations in the scores of individual children indicate the need for the utmost caution in the predictive use of a single test score, or even two such scores" (p. 315).

Critical Thinking Challenges

1. Suppose that a married couple comes to you because you know something about psychology. They tell you that their infant was tested for IQ and scored in the low-normal range. What would you tell them?
2. Imagine the same scenario as in Exercise 1 except that the child is 16 years old. How do you respond to the couple in this case?
3. Suppose that you are called in as a consultant to a school district that wants to use IQ scores to assign children to classes. The district wants to create an above-average class,

an average class, and a below-average class based on the
scores. How would you, as a consultant, react to this plan?

4. Do you believe that the information in this chapter invalidates IQ tests? How does this chapter affect your view of
IQ scores?

5. Does this chapter change your opinion of standardized
tests? If so, how? If we assume that standardized testing is
here to stay, how should we deal with such testing in our
society?

References

Bayley, N. (1966). Learning in adulthood: The role of intelligence. In
H. J. Klausmeier & C. W. Harris (Eds.), *Analyses of concept learning* (pp. 117–138). New York: Academic Press.

Eichorn, D. H., Hunt, J. V., & Honzik, M. P. (1981). Experience, personality, and IQ: Adolescence to middle age. In D. H. Eichorn, J. A.
Clausen, N. Haan, M. P. Honzik, & P. H. Mussen (Eds.), *Present
and past in middle life* (pp. 89–116). New York: Academic Press.

Eichorn, D. H., Mussen, P. H., Clausen, J., Haan, N., & Honzik, M. P.
(1981). Overview. In D. H. Eichorn, J. A. Clausen, N. Haan, M. P.
Honzik, & P. H. Mussen (Eds.), *Present and past in middle life*
(pp. 411–434). New York: Academic Press.

Hindley, C. B., & Owen, C. F. (1978). The extent of individual changes
in I.Q. for ages between 6 months and 17 years, in a British longitudinal sample. *Journal of Child Psychology and Psychiatry, 19,*
329–350.

Honzik, M. P. (1983). Measuring mental abilities in infancy: The value
and limitations. In M. Lewis (Ed.), *Origins of intelligence: Infancy
and early childhood* (2nd ed., pp. 67–105). New York: Plenum.

Honzik, M. P., Macfarlane, J. W., & Allen, L. (1948). The stability of
mental test performance between two and eighteen years. *Journal of Experimental Education, 17,* 309–324.

Kaplan, R. M., & Saccuzzo, D. P. (1997). *Psychological testing: Principles, applications, and issues* (4th ed.). Pacific Grove, CA:
Brooks/Cole.

Lewis, M., & Sullivan, M. W. (1985). Infant intelligence and its assessment. In B. B. Wolman (Ed.), *Handbook of intelligence: Theories,
measurements, and applications* (pp. 505–599). New York:
Wiley.

McCall, R. B., Applebaum, M. I., & Hogarty, P. S. (1973). Developmental changes in mental performance. *Monographs of the Society for
Research in Child Development, 38*(3, Serial No. 150).

Minton, H. L., & Schneider, F. W. (1980). *Differential psychology.*
Monterey, CA: Brooks/Cole.

Rosenthal, R. (1991). Teacher expectancy effects: A brief update 25 years after the Pygmalion experiment. *Journal of Research in Education, 1,* 3–12.

Rosenthal, R., & Jacobson, L. (1968). *Pygmalion in the classroom.* New York: Holt, Rinehart and Winston.

Schaie, K. W. (1983). The Seattle longitudinal study: A 21-year exploration of psychometric intelligence in adulthood. In K. W. Schaie (Ed.), *Longitudinal studies of adult psychological development* (pp. 64–135). New York: Guilford Press.

Schaie, K. W. (1996). *Intellectual development in adulthood: The Seattle longitudinal study.* Cambridge, England: Cambridge University Press.

Shaffer, D. R. (1999). *Developmental psychology: Childhood and adolescence* (5th ed.). Pacific Grove, CA: Brooks/Cole.

Sigelman, C. K. (1999). *Life-span human development* (3rd ed.). Pacific Grove, CA: Brooks/Cole.

10

❦

Understanding Our Own Motives

When psychology professors ask students why they are taking a psychology course, some of the prominent reasons mentioned are "to understand people better," "to find out why people do what they do," and "to discover why people react to me in the ways they do." The common thread in these responses is motivation—trying to determine the reasons or causes behind people's behaviors.

It is interesting that psychologists do not often hear justifications for taking psychology classes such as "to find out why *I* behave the way that *I* do." When we say we're interested in the motives behind other people's behavior, we seem to be making an implicit assumption that we understand the motives behind our own behaviors. We are typically hesitant to admit that we do not know why we did what we did. Let's take a critical look at the preconception that we are aware of our own motivations.

Can We Explain Our Impressions of Other People?

We are constantly forming impressions of people we encounter. We even have a variety of commonsense proverbs that supposedly shed some light on this subject (excuse the sexist language in some of these—people who made up old proverbs were not very gender conscious):

> Beauty is skin deep.
> Clothes make the man.
> Don't judge a book by its cover.
> First impressions are lasting.
> Like father, like son.

Although old proverbs are interesting and even entertaining, they are not based on scientific evidence. What do we know about forming impressions of other people—can we explain the basis on which we judge them?

Landy and Sigall (1974) had college males read essays supposedly written by college females. One-third of the essays had a picture of an attractive "author" attached, one-third had a picture of an unattractive "author," and one-third had no picture. In addition, half of all essays were well written, and half were poorly written. When checking the males' ability to rate the essays, Landy and Sigall found that they did indeed rate good essays higher than poor essays. Evaluations of the essays revealed highest ratings for those supposedly written by attractive authors and lowest ratings for those by unattractive authors, with the "unseen" authors falling between the two groups. The evaluative effect was particularly negative when an unattractive female "wrote" a poor essay. Is attractiveness an important factor in writing good essays? Of course not. But it did affect the evaluation of essays in the study. However, there was an even more important finding. Students also gave overall impressions of the writers' intelligence, sensitivity, and talent (rated only from what the students could see—the essays and the pictures, if any). Again, attractive people were rated more highly than unattractive people. If we asked the students whether attractiveness affected their ratings of the writers, what would they have said? What would you say if asked whether you would let physical attractiveness affect your judgment in such a situation—or in any situation? You wouldn't let attractiveness affect you—or so you would say. Hatfield and Sprecher (1986) noted that although "people generally *say* looks are not too important to them . . . their actions belied their statements" (p. 119).

What happens if experimenters *do* ask people why they evaluated a particular person in a certain way? Nisbett and Wilson (1977a) had students watch a video of a "psychology instructor" and rate him on several dimensions. They saw the instructor in one of two interviews—appearing either warm or cold. Students made ratings of likability, physical appearance, mannerisms, and accent. The interview manipulation worked well as students liked the instructor in the warm interview (5.48 on an 8-point scale) and did not like him in the cold interview (3.18 on the scale). Also, they rated the instructor as more irritating in physical appearance, mannerisms, and accent after seeing him in the cold interview. Because the same person was the subject of both interviews, these ratings *should* have been similar. The experimenters asked some students whether their liking of the instructor had colored their other evaluations. The majority of students, in both the warm and cold conditions, believed that liking had *not* affected their other ratings. Students (in the cold condition) who were asked the opposite question stated that their evaluations of appearance, mannerisms, and accent had decreased their liking of the instructor. It appears they got the relationship backward!

It is abundantly clear that we can and do form impressions of other people. However, we may have trouble explaining *why* we formed the impressions that we did.

Can We Detect Influences on Our Behaviors?

Forming impressions of people is a subjective task, so it may not be surprising that we are unaware of some of the things that influence us. Surely we can look at our own behaviors and explain them—can't we? Maybe not.

In a classic problem-solving study, Maier (1931) asked participants to figure out how to tie two strings together that were hanging from the ceiling. The strings were too far apart to reach both at the same time. The solution involves tying a weight to one string and swinging it like a pendulum, grabbing the second string, and catching the first string when it swings near enough. Maier focused on participants who did not solve the problem immediately and needed a hint. For these 23 people, Maier walked by one string and brushed against it, setting it in motion. Sixteen participants showed an almost-immediate insightful solution (less than 1 minute). However, only 1 of the 16 admitted being influenced by the hint. The other 15 maintained that they did not see the string swing or that they paid no attention to it. These people reported thoughts such as:

> "It just dawned on me."
> "Perhaps a course in physics suggested it to me."
> From a psychology professor: "Having exhausted everything else the next thing was to swing it. I thought of the situation of swinging across a river. I had imagery of monkeys swinging from trees. This imagery appeared simultaneously with the solution. The idea appeared complete." (Maier, 1931, pp. 188–189)

Nisbett and Wilson (1977b) showed students a documentary film. Some heard a loud power saw in the hall during the film. After seeing the film, the students rated it on several dimensions. The experimenters then apologized for the distraction and asked participants whether the noise had affected their ratings. Over half reported that they thought the saw noise had lowered at least one of their ratings. However, comparisons with a control group's ratings showed no differences.

These experiments show how poorly we detect influences on our behaviors. In one case, students denied being influenced when they were. In the other, students believed they were influenced when they were not.

Do Our Verbal Reports and Behaviors Match?

LaPiere (1934) conducted a classic study that led psychologists to question the relationship between what we say and what we do. At a time when racial attitudes in the United States were strongly anti-Chinese, LaPiere took extensive automobile trips with a Chinese couple. LaPiere kept records of the 251 hotels and restaurants they visited during the trip, noting how they were treated. Only once were they refused service or lodging. Afterward, LaPiere wrote to the restaurants and hotels and asked whether they would serve and accept Chinese guests. Of the 128 that responded, over 90% of the proprietors said that they would not serve Chinese.

Storms and Nisbett (1970) worked with insomniacs to determine how verbal reports and behaviors coincided. They gave participants a placebo to take shortly before going to bed, supposedly to study the effect of bodily activity on dreaming. Half the insomniacs were told that the pill would cause arousal (increased heart rate, temperature, and so on) and half were told that the pill would relax them. Arousal participants did report more arousal as a function of the pill than did the relaxation participants. However, when they reported the amount of time they took to fall asleep, the arousal participants had a mean of 41.5 minutes compared to 51.2 minutes for the relaxation participants. Their verbal reports and actual behavior did not match.

Are We Aware That People Influence Our Behavior?

We typically believe that "there is safety in numbers," but the results of a series of helping experiments call that assumption into question. In one experiment, Darley and Latané (1968)

Table 10-1
Effects of Group Size on Likelihood and Speed of Response

Group Size	% Responding by End of Seizure	% Ever Responding	Time until Response (in Seconds)
2 (subject and victim)	85	100	52
3 (subject, victim, and 1 other [perceived])	62	85	93
6 (subject, victim, and 4 others [perceived])	31	62	166

Source: Data from Latané & Darley, 1970, p. 97.

had students participate in a group discussion. Participants were isolated in booths to reduce embarrassment about discussing personal topics (supposedly) but actually so the experimenters could lead participants to believe varying numbers of people were participating in the discussion—two, three, or six. In reality, there were only two participants, the subject and the experimenters' helper (the victim). In the victim's first statement, he talked about difficulty adjusting to college and disclosed that he had epilepsy. After the participant spoke, the victim spoke again and began having a (staged) seizure. The question was how group size would affect helping the victim (see Table 10-1). The results showed that perceived group size inhibited helping the victim. However, participants denied being influenced by the presence of others. Those who believed that other persons were hearing the seizure "reported that they were aware that other people were present, but they felt that this made no difference to their own behavior" (Darley & Latané, 1968, p. 381).

In a similar study, Latané and Rodin (1969) had participants complete a consumer preference questionnaire alone, with another participant (a stranger), or with a friend. While they were working on the questionnaire, they heard a loud crash in another room, followed by the female experimenter's calls for help. The woman was most likely to get help from the solitary participant followed, in order, by the friends, the strangers, and the participant who saw a stranger (a confederate of the experimenter) appear unconcerned. Again, "when subjects were asked whether they had been influenced by the presence or action of their co-workers, they were either unwilling or unable to believe that they had" (Latané & Darley, 1970, p. 65).

Both of these studies show clear-cut evidence that people's helping behavior was reduced by the presence of others. However, the participants stubbornly resisted the implication that they had been influenced by anyone.

Critical Thinking Errors

When we fall prey to thinking that we are aware of our own motivations, we are violating two of our critical thinking guidelines. First, we are not using Guideline 4 (separating fact from opinion) because we are relying on an opinionated view of ourselves. Also, we are ignoring Guideline 6 (using logical inference processes). If we can see that other people don't always know why they behave the way they do, wouldn't it be logical to assume that we also behave in the same manner?

Thinking about Preconceptions

Most of us probably walk around thinking that we understand ourselves—that we know why we do the things we do. In this chapter, we have seen that this simple assumption can be a mistake. It seems that our behaviors are often a product of factors of which we are unaware.

There seems to be an important implication of this finding. If we are uncertain about the causes of our own behavior, we probably should be cautious about drawing conclusions about the behavior of other people. If we want to understand others, it may be crucial to first understand ourselves.

Conclusion

This chapter emphasizes the uncertainty of our motives. Our behaviors are not always linked to our motives and vice versa. It seems that we often may be unclear about the reasons behind our behaviors. Is this the way things always are and always will be? Are we destined to go through life behaving in certain ways for reasons that we don't or can't understand? Fortunately, this pessimistic view is not the entire answer. Although it may be difficult to ascertain a link between motives and behavior, it is not impossible.

There are two simple answers to making our motives more predictive of our behavior. First, we should try to be more aware of our motives. Snyder and Swann (1976) had men pretend to be jurors in a sex-discrimination case. Previously measured attitudes toward affirmative action predicted verdicts only for those men who were asked to think about their attitudes (by giving them "a few minutes to organize your thoughts and views on the affirmative action issue" [p. 1037]) before giving their decision. Second, we need to remember that some motives are more likely to predict behavior than others. Regan and Fazio (1977) measured students' attitudes toward a housing crisis at Cornell University and their behaviors toward alleviating the crisis. Students displaced by the crisis and those not affected showed negative attitudes toward the situation. However, the link between the attitudes and number of actual remedial behaviors (for example, writing letters of protest) was much stronger for the affected group than the nonaffected group. Thus, attitudes (or motives) forged through actual experience are more predictive of later behavior. Myers (1999) also noted that, compared to attitudes we form passively, experiential attitudes "are more thoughtful, more certain, more stable, more resistant to attack, more accessible, and more emotionally charged" (p. 136).

The message of this chapter is fairly simple—you may be mistaken about the motives behind some of your behaviors. However, if you think about your motives and try to rely on your *own* motives, the link should be clearer.

Critical Thinking Challenges

1. Why do you think we are much more likely to wonder about other people's motives than about our own? Give three reasons. Try to find data to support your ideas.

2. Experimental data strongly support the notion of a physical attractiveness stereotype in which we attribute many positive characteristics to physically attractive people. Why would we behave in this manner? Can you explain the motive behind this stereotype?

3. This chapter presents a multitude of studies that imply we are not always clear about our motivations. Is this uncertainty in some way adaptive? Develop a hypothetical reason why this would be true.

4. Given your three hypotheses from Exercise 3, design an experiment that would allow you to test the hypothesis that you believe is most likely correct.

5. In the conclusion section, you read about Snyder and Swann's (1976) research. Their findings imply that our motives will predict our behavior more accurately if we think about our motives before acting. Why would we act *without* thinking about our motives or attitudes? Is there any logical explanation possible?

References

Darley, J. M., & Latané, B. (1968). Bystander intervention in emergencies: Diffusion of responsibility. *Journal of Personality and Social Psychology, 8,* 377–383.

Hatfield, E., & Sprecher, S. (1986). *Mirror, mirror: The importance of looks in everyday life.* Albany, NY: SUNY Press.

Landy, D., & Sigall, H. (1974). Beauty is talent: Task evaluation as a function of the performer's physical attractiveness. *Journal of Personality and Social Psychology, 29,* 299–304.

LaPiere, R. T. (1934). Attitudes vs. actions. *Social Forces, 13,* 230–237.

Latané, B., & Darley, J. M. (1970). *The unresponsive bystander: Why doesn't he help?* New York: Appleton-Century-Crofts.

Latané, B., & Rodin, J. (1969). A lady in distress: Inhibiting effects of friends and strangers on bystander intervention. *Journal of Experimental Social Psychology, 5,* 189–202.

Maier, N. R. F. (1931). Reasoning in humans. II. The solution of a problem and its appearance in consciousness. *Journal of Comparative Psychology, 12,* 181–194.

Myers, D. G. (1999). *Social psychology* (6th ed.). New York: McGraw-Hill.

Nisbett, R. E., & Wilson, T. D. (1977a). The halo effect: Evidence for unconscious alteration of judgments. *Journal of Personality and Social Psychology, 35,* 250–256.

Nisbett, R. E., & Wilson, T. D. (1977b). Telling more than we can know: Verbal reports on mental processes. *Psychological Review, 84,* 231–259.

Regan, D. T., & Fazio, R. (1977). On the consistency between attitudes and behavior: Look to the method of attitude formation. *Journal of Experimental Social Psychology, 13,* 28–45.

Snyder, M., & Swann, W. B., Jr. (1976). When actions reflect attitudes: The politics of impression management. *Journal of Personality and Social Psychology, 34,* 1034–1042.

Storms, M. D., & Nisbett, R. E. (1970). Insomnia and the attribution process. *Journal of Personality and Social Psychology, 16,* 319–328.

11

🌿

Evaluating Codependency

An interesting trend in recent years is the tendency for classifications of "abnormal" behavior to begin in popular rather than scientific literature. Although this evolutionary pattern causes some concern due to potential problems with popular literature (see Chapters 2 and 12), as critical thinkers we should not immediately dismiss an idea merely because of its origin. Instead, we should use our guidelines for critical thinking to evaluate new ideas and positions. In this chapter, we will examine the developing "disorder" of codependency.

The first recognition of codependency is difficult to track down. It appears to have arisen from work with families of alcoholics with a minor problem known as co-alcoholism (Beattie, 1987; Lyon & Greenberg, 1991). In its original manifestation, codependency referred to people who became entangled with an addict in such a way that their behavior actually maintained or encouraged the addictive behavior (Lyon & Greenberg, 1991). For example, a spouse might attempt to help the alcoholic by lying to the alcoholic's boss, by paying unpaid bills, by cleaning or fixing messes made by the alcoholic, and so on. Thus, the alcoholic would not have to face the unpleasant consequences of his or her behavior, and the destructive behavior pattern would be maintained (Haaken, 1990).

Scope of Codependency

In the late 1980s, codependency was more broadly defined. Beattie (1987) defined a codependent as "one who has let another person's behavior affect him or her, and who is obsessed with controlling that person's behavior" (p. 31). Whitfield (1991) defined codependence as a "condition manifested by any suffering and dysfunction that is associated with or due to focusing on the needs and behavior of others" (p. 8). Whitfield also reviewed 22 additional definitions of the concept. Beattie (1987) listed 234 symptoms of codependency and even said that list was not all-inclusive!

The concept of codependency has also been broadly applied. Beattie (1987) wrote her book about codependency for persons with a variety of problems: "Whether the person you've let yourself be affected by is an alcoholic, gambler, foodaholic, workaholic, sexaholic, criminal, rebellious teenager, neurotic parent, another codependent, or any combination of the above, this book is for you" (p. 6). Because she applied the term so broadly, Beattie estimated that 80,000,000 Americans were probably codependent. To Beattie's list of addictions, Schaef (1987) added drugs, nicotine, caffeine, sugar, salt, accumulating money, religion, and worry. Thus, it seems that virtually everyone is a candidate for codependency. Kaminer, in a book that is generally critical of pop psychology, noted that "almost everyone—96 percent of all Americans—suffers from codependency, experts assert, and given their very broad definitions of this disease, we probably do" (1992, p. 10). A critical thinker might note that one criterion for abnormality is a "response that is not typical or culturally expected" (Durand & Barlow, 2000, p. 2). Therefore if many or most Americans experience codependency, by definition, it is not abnormal.

Persons at Risk for Codependency

In its original context of being alcohol-related, codependency was mostly applied to females as the wives of alcoholics (Beattie, 1987; Lyon & Greenberg, 1991). In similar fashion, Schaef (1987) equated addicts with her "White Male System" and codependence with her "Reactive Female System." Although many of the codependents described in books are males, the target market for those books is females, as one publisher estimated that the audience is 85% female (Kaminer, 1992). Wright and Wright (1991) believe that much of the background for codependency came from Norwood's popular book *Women Who Love Too Much* (1985). Kaminer postulated that codependency is primarily a female problem because women have traditionally been given the responsibility for maintaining the emotional balance of the family. A critical thinker cannot eliminate codependence as an abnormal behavior because of the alleged gender difference. Many abnormal behaviors do show different rates of incidence as a function of gender (e.g., depression, eating disorders, substance abuse disorders).

What Behavior Signals Codependency?

Given some of the statistics quoted earlier, it might be easier to ask "What behavior is *not* codependent?" Nevertheless, rather than trying to define the term by exclusion, let's look at some of the most telling characteristics of codependents. On the cover of Beattie's (1987) book, four questions are asked of prospective readers to help them decide whether they had a codependency problem. These questions help summarize the concept briefly.

- Have you become so absorbed in other people's problems that you don't have time to identify, or solve, your own?
- Do you care so deeply about other people that you've forgotten how to care for yourself?
- Do you need to control events and people around you because you feel everything around and inside you is out of control?
- Do you feel responsible for so much because the people around you feel responsible for so little?

Of course, for a behavior pattern to be considered abnormal, a formal set of diagnostic criteria must be developed. Cermak (1986) proposed just such a set of criteria for codependency, hoping the disorder would be considered for inclusion in a future edition of the *Diagnostic and Statistical Manual of Mental Disorders (DSM)*. His list included:

- continual investment of self-esteem in the ability to influence/control feelings and behavior in self and others in the face of obvious adverse consequences;
- assumption of responsibility for meeting others' needs to the exclusion of acknowledging one's own needs;
- anxiety and boundary distortions in situations of intimacy and separation;
- enmeshment in relationships with personality disordered, drug dependent and impulse disordered individuals; and

- exhibits (in any combination of three of more) constriction of emotions with or without dramatic outbursts, depression, hypervigilance, compulsions, anxiety, excessive reliance on denial, substance abuse, recurrent physical or sexual abuse, stress-related medical illnesses, and/or a primary relationship with an active substance abuser for at least two years without seeking outside support. (Cermak, 1986, pp. 16-17)

However, despite this and other calls for codependency to be listed as a diagnosable mental disorder, the latest version of the *DSM* (American Psychiatric Association, 2000) does not include codependency. This fact is difficult for a critical thinker to ignore.

Consequences of Codependency

Beattie's questions and Cermak's criteria highlight most of the characteristics of codependents that Beattie (1987) identified in her book: caretaking, low self-worth, repression, obsession, control, denial, dependency, poor communication, weak boundaries, lack of trust, anger, and sex problems. Kaminer (1992) noted that codependency has been blamed for drug abuse, alcoholism, anorexia, child abuse, compulsive gambling, chronic lateness, fear of intimacy, and low self-esteem. Whitfield (1991) listed numbness to emotional pain, inability to grieve, compulsive behaviors, mood swings, and chronic unhappiness as psychological outcomes of codependency and maintained that it can even lead to physical problems, particularly chronic fatigue syndrome. It is not unusual for a mental disorder to have far-reaching consequences and effects. Thus, this extensive list of consequences is not adequate justification for a critical thinker to rule out codependency as a legitimate disorder.

Research Evidence Concerning Codependency

Several years after codependency came into vogue, little research existed to support the concept (Fischer, Spann, & Crawford, 1991; Wright & Wright, 1991). Wright and Wright (1991) characterized the codependency literature as ranging "from the popular to the semi-scholarly" (p. 435). O'Brien and Gaborit (1992) believed that the disorder received a great deal of attention from self-help groups and mental health workers in the chemical-dependency field, but little scrutiny from clinical psychologists, who would be more likely to conduct experimental studies of such a phenomenon. One research approach to any hypothesized disorder is to develop a measure or measures of that disorder. Currently, many years after the concept of codependency developed, there is not an agreed-upon way to define or measure the concept. For example, Martin and Piazza (1995) tested 207 women diagnosed as codependent with a well-known personality inventory (the MMPI). They found that the women's scores fell within the normal range and that there was no distinguishable pattern to their personality profiles.

Although there are experimental studies dealing with codependency, the results are mixed. For every study that provides empirical support for the concept, there seems to be another that does not. For example, Lyon and Greenberg (1991) found that female offspring of alcoholic parents (operationally defined as codependents in this study) offered more help to an exploitive experimenter than to a nurturant experimenter. In addition, they also liked the exploitive experimenter more than a control group (with nonalcoholic parents) did. These "codependents" also rated their alcoholic fathers more highly than they did their mothers. Lyon and Greenberg hypothesized that these women believed the exploitive experimenter needed more nurturance than did the nurturant experimenter, and therefore they reacted favorably toward him, just as they did toward their fathers.

On the other hand, Cullen and Carr (1999) used a popular codependency scale to classify their 284 participants as codependent or not codependent. They failed to confirm their hypothesis that the codependent group would report a greater incidence of parental drug and alcohol abuse or of abuse as children. Of course, it is important for a critical thinker to know that empirical evidence (on any topic) is mixed.

Critical Evaluation of Codependency

Recognizing codependency as a new disorder has raised some problems. First and foremost, there is the problem of defining the concept—Harper and Capdevila (1990) said that no two authors used the same definition, so confusion reigns supreme. For example, in the research cited earlier, Lyon and Greenberg

(1991) defined a codependent as anyone who had an alcoholic parent. In contrast, Cullen and Carr (1999) found codependency to be independent of parental chemical dependency. Without a consistent definition, it is impossible to list codependency as a disorder.

Second, little research evidence exists to confirm the disorder. Much of the information about codependency comes from more informal sources such as casual observations or self-help groups. We must beware of the power of expectations—if we expect to see examples of a disorder, we probably will. Third, codependency almost seems to serve a garbage can function—"let's throw everything in here." With Beattie's 234 symptoms, Beattie's and Schaef's lists of addictions, and estimates of those with codependency ranging as high as 96% of Americans, the concept of codependency starts to lose meaning. If codependency is used to explain everything, then it doesn't really explain anything. Fourth, some writers criticize codependency as being sexist because it is applied primarily to females. Van Wormer (1989) maintained that codependency is used to blame the victim. For example, rather than accepting responsibility for his behavior, the alcoholic husband can now argue that his codependent wife drove him to drink.

Critical Thinking Errors

At this time, accepting codependency as a mental disorder appears problematical. Guideline 3 (maintaining a skeptical attitude) and Guideline 7 (examining available evidence before drawing conclusions) seem to be violated. As we have seen, there is little conclusive evidence to support this concept. When little evidence exists, we should remain skeptical and continue to ask for good, convincing evidence.

Thinking about Preconceptions

It appears that a sizable segment of the self-help industry is operating on some strong preconceptions about codependency. The number of people who have jumped on the bandwagon without much empirical support is surprising. When a person who believes that codependency is a real phenomenon observes that phenomenon where he or she expects it to occur, we may be dealing with self-fulfilling prophecy, stereotyping, or bias of some other type.

What about you? I would guess that many readers know someone who has been diagnosed as codependent or is a self-proclaimed codependent. Have you heard about and read about this problem so much that you have already decided it does exist, or do you still have an open mind, ready to continue critically evaluating new evidence?

Conclusion

Remember that critical thinking does not always guarantee a definite conclusion. Guideline 1 reminds us that we must sometimes deal with ambiguity and uncertainty. The situation regarding codependency is quite similar to what we observed about hypnotically aided memory in Chapter 6. Although there is little empirical evidence to support the clear-cut and definitive existence of codependency, the jury is still out. Codependency is still a relatively recent phenomenon, so it is possible that some of the problems we reviewed earlier will be answered in the future through research. At this point, it seems safest to withhold judgment but remember to use our critical thinking guidelines when we read about codependency.

Critical Thinking Challenges

1. This chapter implies that there is a problem with a new behavior disorder originating from popular sources rather than from more scientific sources. Give three reasons why this is so.
2. What kind of problem is created when multiple definitions of a single concept exist? In particular, how do multiple definitions impede the recognition of codependency as a mental disorder?
3. Do you think that any problem can be recognized as a mental disorder if it disproportionally affects one sex or the other? Why or why not? Should sexual politics be an issue in determining mental disorders?
4. What would you want to see as evidence before voting to include codependency as a mental disorder in the *DSM*? Why is it important to have evidence backing the inclusion of disorders in the *DSM*?

5. Imagine that you are designing an experimental study dealing with codependency. What questions would you want to ask and why? How would you design your study?

References

American Psychiatric Association. (2000). *Diagnostic and statistical manual of mental disorders (DSM-IV-TR)* (4th ed., text revision). Washington, DC: Author.

Beattie, M. (1987). *Codependent no more.* New York: HarperCollins.

Cermak, T. L. (1986). Diagnostic criteria for codependency. *Journal of Psychoactive Drugs, 18,* 15–20.

Cullen, J., & Carr, A. (1999). Codependency: An empirical study from a systemic perspective. *Contemporary Family Therapy, 21,* 505–526.

Durand, V. M., & Barlow, D. H. (2000). *Abnormal psychology: An introduction* (2nd ed.). Belmont, CA: Wadsworth.

Fischer, J. L., Spann, L., & Crawford, D. (1991). Measuring codependency. *Alcoholism Treatment Quarterly, 8,* 87–100.

Haaken, J. (1990). A critical analysis of the co-dependence construct. *Psychiatry, 53,* 396–406.

Harper, J., & Capdevila, C. (1990). Codependency: A critique. *Journal of Psychoactive Drugs, 22,* 285–292.

Kaminer, W. (1992). *I'm dysfunctional, you're dysfunctional: The recovery movement and other self-help fashions.* Reading, MA: Addison-Wesley.

Lyon, D., & Greenberg, J. (1991). Evidence of codependency in women with an alcoholic parent: Helping out Mr. Wrong. *Journal of Personality and Social Psychology, 61,* 435–439.

Martin, A. L., & Piazza, N. J. (1995). Codependency in women: Personality disorder or popular descriptive term? *Journal of Mental Health Counseling, 17,* 428–440.

Norwood, R. (1985). *Women who love too much.* New York: Pocket Books.

O'Brien, P. E., & Gaborit, M. (1992). Codependency: A disorder separate from chemical dependency. *Journal of Clinical Psychology, 48,* 129–136.

Schaef, A. W. (1987). *When society becomes an addict.* San Francisco: Harper & Row.

van Wormer, K. (1989). Co-dependency: Implications for women and therapy. *Women & Therapy, 8,* 51–63.

Whitfield, C. L. (1991). *Co-dependence: Healing the human condition.* Deerfield Beach, FL: Health Communications.

Wright, P. H., & Wright, K. D. (1991). Codependency: Addictive love, adjustive relating, or both? *Contemporary Family Therapy, 13,* 435–454.

12

🌿

Is Bibliotherapy Helpful?

In any bookstore at any shopping mall look for the self-help section. Unless you regularly browse in this section, you will probably be startled at the number and variety of self-help books available. Although it may not surprise you to find books on topics such as weight loss, smoking, parenting, and sexual problems, finding books covering complex psychological topics such as depression, phobias, codependency, and childhood sexual abuse ought to make you stop and think. Have we become so sophisticated with our therapeutic approaches that we can now dispense help from a book rather than a face-to-face meeting with a trained professional? In this chapter, we will examine the trend toward bibliotherapy.

You might ask whether this trend is really worth examining—is the self-help phenomenon actually that widespread? Barrera, Rosen, and Glasgow (1981) cited estimates from the 1970s of over 100 weight-control books and over 200 child-care books on the market. In 1988, one publisher guessed that over 2000 self-help books were being published annually (Doheny, 1988), so the 1970s estimates are probably very low now. In addition, the production of self-help audiocassettes is now popular—you can probably find those at your local mall bookstore also. One company increased their sales of subliminal tapes tenfold in a 2-year period to over $6 million in 1988 (Lofflin, 1988). Jacobs and Goodman (1989) estimated that over 6 million American adults were involved in self-help groups in 1987. Finally, we know that self-help is an integral part of American culture when we see it parodied on *Saturday Night Live* and other comedy shows.

Potential Benefits of Self-Help Therapy

Let's examine why bibliotherapy has grown to be a powerful force. What benefits make bibliotherapy so attractive? According to Barrera et al. (1981), four major benefits exist.

1. If self-help strategies are used, the *range of services can be expanded*. Therapists can reduce the time spent with some clients so that others can be reached.
2. Bibliotherapy can *educate consumers about psychotherapy*. Barrera et al. cited several studies showing that people entering therapy have better outcomes if they have learned pretherapy information that can be contained in a book.
3. Bibliotherapy may help in *maintaining treatment effects*. To avoid relapse after therapy, a client can continue to read and work on material provided in a manual.
4. Bibliotherapy can help in *prevention*. If people read self-help books routinely, some problems may never develop—an inoculation strategy.

With this impressive list of potential benefits, it is hard to imagine that there are also potential risks—but there are.

Potential Risks of Self-Help Therapy

Barrera et al. (1981) pointed out that traditional therapy is not without its risks. For example, it is not a given that everyone who undergoes therapy will either improve or even stay the same—evidence of deterioration effects has also been found. Thus, it is important to scrutinize self-help approaches as rigorously as standard therapeutic methods. Barrera et al. cited three potential risks of bibliotherapy.

1. In traditional therapy, the first step is an assessment by a trained professional. In self-help approaches, *improper assessment* is a possibility. Particularly troublesome would be a person who attempts self-help when the problem is too severe for such a strategy or when the problem is physical rather than psychological in nature. In addition, some self-help strategies are designed to help change the behavior of another person (for example, child management books) and, thus, extend the problem of improper assessment to someone else.

2. Even if the assessment is proper, then the risk of *prescribing treatment methods* arises. Perhaps even more than with therapy, a myriad of self-help approaches exist. How can a consumer choose which approach would work best for a particular problem?

3. Finally, one must face the risk of *failure* with a self-help approach. The peril here is that there is no therapist present to suggest alternative strategies or refer the patient elsewhere. The consumer must bear the burden of failure alone, which may worsen the problem.

Do these risks outweigh the benefits? This question is impossible to answer in any general sense without looking at some evidence. Without examining relevant research, we are likely to draw a conclusion based solely on our preconceptions.

Claims of Self-Help Books

Many of the claims about benefits of self-help books come from the books themselves. Unfortunately, much of the "evidence" for these claims appears on the covers and dust jackets of the books rather than inside the books. Gerald Rosen called for empirical validation of self-help approaches as early as 1976. Rosen was pessimistic about the prospects of such validation, noting that programs were already being marketed without being tested. In a cynical vein, he wrote that "at the present time, the only contingencies that need affect the sale of these materials are monetary ones" (1976, p. 140).

In 1987, Rosen cited an example of a self-help book by Mahoney and Mahoney (1976a) titled *Permanent Weight Control*. Yet in the same year, the Mahoneys published a scholarly review paper on obesity (1976b), stating, "We remain a long way away from any semblance of justification for complacency in weight regulation. Significant poundage losses are still in the minority and long-term maintenance has remained seldom examined" (p. 30). In a letter of response, Mahoney (1988) admitted that he had learned "quite a bit about the Madison Avenue side of psychology" (p. 598) and that, in his opinion, there was "no denying the powerful role that commercial factors (usually emphasized by the publisher) have come to play in the titling, packaging, and marketing of self-help books" (p. 598).

Rosen (1988) reviewed another self-help book, *Mind Power: Getting What You Want through Mental Training* (Zilbergeld & Lazarus, 1987), and found its claims extravagant. According to the book's dust jacket:

> In this remarkable book, two internationally acclaimed clinical psychologists have combined their professional expertise to provide clear strategies and nuts-and-bolts techniques that can give you new power over your life. . . . *Mind Power* is the first book to show you how easy it can be to use these techniques to set goals, reduce stress, and increase performance, creativity and productivity—in other words, to help you shape your life into what you wish it to be. (cited in Rosen, 1988, p. 861)

Rosen (1988) noted that *Mind Power* covered topics such as shyness, weight loss, sexual anxiety, fear reduction, assertiveness, and sports performance. However, in evaluating the book's techniques, Rosen found evidence only of informal feedback without clinical research. Thus, he described *Mind Power* as "just another untested book on the topic of hypnotic self-suggestions and imagery techniques" (p. 862).

Empirical Evidence Concerning Self-Help Books

Two early reviews examined self-help books and their evaluations. Glasgow and Rosen (1978) reviewed 86 behaviorally oriented self-help programs or manuals and found 74 evaluative studies or case reports, for a 86% evaluation rate. In a review of an additional two years' worth of books (Glasgow & Rosen, 1979), they found an additional 73 programs, but only 43 evaluative reports, for a 59% rate. They found that 53% of the programs had not been evaluated at all. Glasgow and Rosen (1979) called for increased emphasis on program evaluations. However, after almost 15 years, Rosen (1993) still found that "the majority of do-it-yourself treatments have never been assessed" (p. 341). In both the 1978 and the 1979 reviews, Glasgow and Rosen found that some self-help programs produced beneficial effects, although the persistence of such effects was somewhat problematical. Some programs seemed to require at least a minimal amount of therapist assistance.

Scogin, Bynum, Stephens, and Calhoon (1990) reviewed 40 articles that compared self-administered programs to other types of treatment. They found that self-administered treatments produced effects that were superior to no treatment ($n = 17$) and that were no different from therapist-administered treatments ($n = 10$). Starker (1988) surveyed 121 psychologists in Boston and San Diego about self-help books. The results showed that 73 (60.3%) prescribed self-help books to supplement their treatment, albeit only 7 did so regularly and 9 did so frequently. Although these two studies showed encouraging results, the numbers of programs evaluated and psychologists surveyed are quite small.

Failures of Specific Self-Help Programs

Let's review a few specific instances of what can go wrong with self-help programs. This section is meant not to be an indictment of all self-help programs, but merely to provide some examples.

Programs successfully administered by a therapist may not be successfully self-administered. Matson and Ollendick (1977) evaluated Azrin and Foxx's *Toilet Training in Less Than a Day* (1974). Five mothers attempted to train their child using only the book, and five used the book plus an experienced trainer who was available for supervision and prompting. The results showed that four of five mothers who had the trainer were successful whereas only one of five who used the book alone succeeded. In a similar study treating premature ejaculation, Zeiss (1978) reported successful results for six of six couples receiving therapist-administered treatment, for five of six couples who used a self-help manual in conjunction with phone calls from a therapist, and zero of six couples who used only the self-help manual.

Failed self-help efforts may make the problem worse or create a new problem. Matson and Ollendick (1977) reported that children who failed to be potty trained evidenced tantrums and avoidance behavior to a greater degree than children who were trained. Brownell, Heckerman, and Westlake (1978) found minimal weight loss for participants using only a self-help manual for dieting. Because of the emotional and physical hazards of unsuccessful dieting, they concluded that "it is possible that an ineffective diet is more dangerous than no diet" (p. 594).

Small changes in tested self-help programs may have important implications. Rosen, Glasgow, and Barrera (1976) developed a program to help clients overcome their snake phobias. Clients who completed a completely self-administered program progressed as much as those who were in therapist-administered or self-administered groups with minimal thera-pist contact. However, only 50% of the self-administered group finished the program. In a follow-up study, Barrera and Rosen (1977) attempted to increase compliance by combining a self-reward contract with the self-administered program. If partici-pants did their homework for the week, they were to reward themselves. Again, 50% of a self-administered group completed the program, but *none* of the participants in the reward group finished. Thus, the behavioral manipulation designed to in-crease compliance completely backfired.

Critical Thinking Errors

The major problems with critical thinking in taking self-help books at face value are in Guideline 3 (maintaining an air of skepticism) and Guideline 7 (examining available evidence). Be-cause there seems to be little skepticism from consumers regard-ing these books, there is little evidence to be examined. Unfortu-nately, few studies have been conducted to test these books. If the general public became somewhat more skeptical, the authors would begin testing the empirical validity of their claims.

Thinking about Preconceptions

Have you ever bought (or read) a self-help book? A self-help tape or subliminal suggestion tape? Have you ever thought about buying such a book or tape but consciously rejected that notion? Either way, you were probably acting on a preconceived notion that the book or tape would or would not help you. Be-cause of your preconception, could you really give the book or tape a fair chance?

Conclusion

This chapter brings us to some uncertain conclusions. Are self-help books helpful? Possibly. Are *all* self-help books beneficial? Probably not. Are *all* self-help books a waste of time and money? Probably not.

What should we conclude about self-help books? Per-haps the safest conclusion is *not* to draw a general conclusion.

Contemporary Psychology (CP) is a journal of reviews of psychology books. In 1981, *CP's* editor, Donald J. Foss, wrote that *CP* had not previously included self-help book reviews but was beginning to do so. Because Gerald Rosen had chaired the APA Task Force on Self-Help Therapies, he was chosen to develop guidelines for such reviews and to work with *CP* as an advisory editor. Although Rosen published his list of guidelines for reviewing self-help books (1981), some of the guidelines also seem appropriate for evaluating self-help approaches on a case-by-case basis:

- Has the author attempted to convey accurate information regarding empirical support for the program, and has the author determined if readers develop accurate expectations?
- Does the book provide a basis for self-diagnosis (in the sense of a reader determining appropriate applications), and have the methods for self-diagnosis been evaluated?
- Have the techniques that are presented in the book received empirical support?
- Has the book itself been tested for its clinical efficiency, and under what conditions of usage have the tests been conducted?
- In light of the above points, what is the accuracy of any claims made in the title or content of the book?
- Can comparisons be made between the book under review and other books on the same or related topics? (Rosen, 1981, p. 190)

These guidelines should allow a consumer to evaluate any self-help book, cassette, or treatment plan objectively. Just as one would not take an untested medicine, neither should a critical consumer begin an untested self-help program.

Critical Thinking Challenges

1. Find information about the placebo effect and self-fulfilling prophecy. How might these concepts be relevant to self-help programs?
2. Richard Rosen wrote a book titled *Psychobabble* (1977). Rosen used the term *psychobabble* to refer to "popular catchphrases of revelation" (p. 3) that seem to contain meaning but are actually empty and meaningless. Throughout his book, Rosen cited examples such as "getting in

touch with yourself," "becoming fully aware," "I'm really into myself right now," and so on. Could the term *psycho-babble* be extended to self-help programs? Why or why not?

3. In the section concerning empirical evidence for self-help books, Starker's (1988) survey of psychologists who recommend such books was mentioned. Generate three hypotheses concerning why so many psychologists suggest these books to their clients. Which hypothesis do you favor? Why?

4. Suppose you talk to a psychology major who tells you that he wants to major in psychology to help people but isn't interested in "all that research stuff." Based on the information in this chapter, what would you tell him?

5. Go to your school library or a public library and find a self-help book. Using information from this chapter, evaluate the book and its program. Would you recommend this book to someone who needed help? Why or why not?

References

Azrin, N. H., & Foxx, R. M. (1974). *Toilet training in less than a day.* New York: Simon & Schuster.

Barrera, M., Jr., & Rosen, G. M. (1977). Detrimental effects of a self-reward contracting program on subjects' involvement in self-administered desensitization. *Journal of Consulting and Clinical Psychology, 45,* 1180–1181.

Barrera, M., Jr., Rosen, G. M., & Glasgow, R. E. (1981). Rights, risks, and responsibilities in the use of self-help psychotherapy. In G. T. Hannah, W. P. Christian, & H. B. Clark (Eds.), *Preservation of client rights* (pp. 204–220). New York: Free Press.

Brownell, K. D., Heckerman, C. L., & Westlake, R. J. (1978). Therapist and group contact as variables in the behavioral treatment of obesity. *Journal of Consulting and Clinical Psychology, 46,* 593–594.

Doheny, K. (1988, October 2). Self-help. *The Los Angeles Times,* Part IV, pp. 1, 8.

Foss, D. J. (1981). CP speaks. *Contemporary Psychology, 26,* 189.

Glasgow, R. E., & Rosen, G. M. (1978). Behavioral bibliotherapy: A review of self-help behavior therapy manuals. *Psychological Bulletin, 85,* 1–23.

Glasgow, R. E., & Rosen, G. M. (1979). Self-help behavior therapy manuals: Recent developments and clinical usage. *Clinical Behavior Therapy Review, 1,* (1) 3–20.

Jacobs, M. K., & Goodman, G. (1989). Psychology and self-help groups: Predictions on a partnership. *American Psychologist, 44,* 536–545.

Lofflin, J. (1988, March 20). Help from the hidden persuaders. *New York Times,* Sec. III, p. 17.

Mahoney, M. J. (1988). Beyond the self-help prolemics. *American Psychologist, 43,* 598–599.

Mahoney, M. J., & Mahoney, B. K. (1976a). *Permanent weight control.* New York: W. W. Norton.

Mahoney, M. J., & Mahoney, K. (1976b). Treatment of obesity: A clinical exploration. In B. J. Williams, S. Martin, & J. P. Foreyt (Eds.), *Obesity: Behavioral approaches to dietary management* (pp. 30–39). New York: Brunner/Mazel.

Matson, J. L., & Ollendick, T. H. (1977). Issues in toilet training normal children. *Behavior Therapy, 8,* 549–553.

Rosen, G. M. (1976). The development and use of nonprescription behavior therapies. *American Psychologist, 31,* 139–141.

Rosen, G. M. (1981). Guidelines for the review of do-it-yourself treatment books. *Contemporary Psychology, 26,* 189–191.

Rosen, G. M. (1987). Self-help treatment books and the commercialization of psychotherapy. *American Psychologist, 42,* 46–51.

Rosen, G. M. (1988). Multimodal marketing: The selling of *Mind Power. Contemporary Psychology, 33,* 861–863.

Rosen, G. M. (1993). Self-help or hype? Comments on psychology's failure to advance self-care. *Professional Psychology: Research and Practice, 24,* 340–345.

Rosen, G. M., Glasgow, R. E., & Barrera, M., Jr. (1976). A controlled study to assess the clinical efficacy of totally self-administered systematic desensitization. *Journal of Consulting and Clinical Psychology, 44,* 208–217.

Rosen, R. D. (1977). *Psychobabble.* New York: Atheneum.

Scogin, F., Bynum, J., Stephens, G., & Calhoon, S. (1990). Efficacy of self-administered treatment programs: Meta-analytic review. *Professional Psychology: Research and Practice, 21,* 42–47.

Starker, S. (1988). Do-it-yourself therapy: The prescription of self-help books by psychologists. *Psychotherapy, 25,* 142–146.

Zeiss, R. A. (1978). Self-directed treatment for premature ejaculation. *Journal of Consulting and Clinical Psychology, 46,* 1234–1241.

Zilbergeld, B., & Lazarus, A. A. (1987). *Mind power: Getting what you want through mental training.* Boston: Little, Brown.

13

𝖶

Social Influence Tactics

From childhood we are constantly bombarded by attempts to influence us through advertising. Myers (1999) estimated that children view about 20,000 television commercials a year, so the potential for being influenced is astronomical. We see how easily swayed children are as they ask for McDonalds' Happy Meals, Disney toys, or the latest Barbie accessory because they saw these products advertised on television. As adults, we believe that we are immune to such blatant attempts to manipulate us. However, not all influence attempts are so obvious. Robert Cialdini, a noted social psychologist, posed as a prospective employee and spent time in sales trainee meetings and in advertising, public relations, and fund-raising agencies to learn their persuasive tactics. Cialdini (2001) summarized several principles of social influence used by such organizations. Let's look behind the scenes at these "sneaky" tactics used to bring about compliance.

Authority

Many people elicit a high degree of compliance because of their positions as teachers, parents, police officers, or other figures of authority. Advertising campaigns often rely heavily on authorities in communicating their messages. Certainly Shaquille O'Neal is an expert basketball player and knows a great deal about basketball shoes. Why should we listen to him, though, when he tries to sell us breakfast cereal or hamburgers?

In research to test medical doctors' influence, Hofling and colleagues (1966) phoned nurses at a hospital and, posing as unidentified "physicians," ordered that a certain drug be given to a patient. This situation violated several principles of good hospital care: The order was not given in person, the person giving the order was unknown to the nurse, the drug amount prescribed was twice the maximum daily dose, and the drug was not cleared for use in the hospital. Nonetheless, 21 of 22 nurses were on their way to the patient's room to administer the drug when they were stopped.

We have also learned to respect people in uniforms. Sometimes this respect generalizes to create unnecessary social influence. Bickman (1974) had a person stop a pedestrian to ask for a dime for a parking meter. The person was dressed either in street clothes or in a security guard's uniform. Most of the pedestrians (76%) complied with the request of the person in a uniform; only 30% complied when the person was dressed in street clothes. We can be influenced by someone in authority without even realizing it.

Foot in the Door

Some influencers use the *foot-in-the-door* technique, in which the requester persuades someone to comply with a small request first and then follows up with a larger request. So, to put Mom or Dad in a giving mood, you might first ask for $5 and later conveniently remember that you need $20 rather than $5. This technique of "priming the pump" appears to be a favorite among salespeople and advertising campaigns. Have you ever noticed the advertising come-ons that offer you a free gift if you test drive a car or look at some real estate property? These are attempts to get a "foot in the door"—a time-honored tactic of door-to-door salespeople who believe that if they can get inside a person's house, then the sale is as good as made.

Cialdini (2001) noted that influence in such situations is driven by our need to be consistent once we have made a commitment. Freedman and Fraser (1966) had people ask homeowners to post a large, poorly lettered DRIVE CAREFULLY sign in their front yards. Only 17% were willing to do so. Another group of homeowners was asked to display a 3-inch-square BE A SAFE DRIVER sign; many were willing to do so. This second group was later asked to display the large, ugly sign in their yards; 76% agreed to do so. Because they had made a prior commitment to safe driving, they agreed to the second request to remain consistent.

Liking

There is a multitude of evidence that indicates we like people who are similar to us. Thus, if a salesperson is similar to us (or can convince us of a similarity), we are more likely to buy the offered product. The administration at each college you may have visited before your college career wanted you to like the person who hosted you so that you would be more likely to make their college your first choice. So athletes often host prospects who are athletes, honors students host prospects who are bright, members of the band host prospects who are interested in the band, and so on.

Crandall (1988) measured friendship patterns within two sororities and assessed binge eating (uncontrollable urges to consume large quantities of food). Not surprisingly, Crandall found that stable friendship groups emerged during the year. What might surprise you is that these friendship groups were more similar in their binge patterns at the end of the year than at the beginning. The finding was *not* that people with similar binge patterns became friends, but that friends developed similar binge patterns. Thus, liking influenced behavior.

Janis, Kaye, and Kirschner (1965) had two groups of participants read persuasive messages. One group snacked on peanuts and soft drinks while reading; the others did not drink or eat. The snacking group was influenced more than the group that simply read the messages. It appears that we should beware of organizations that offer us complimentary banquets during fund-raising drives! Perhaps this is the origin of the saying, "There's no such thing as a free lunch."

Reciprocation

The informal norm of reciprocity is learned in childhood. Various groups who want your money have known this principle for years. How often have you received a relatively worthless gift (a flower from the Hare Krishnas in the airport or address labels from some charity group) that was followed by a solicitation? Following the rules of polite society, you then felt obligated to return the favor, and so you often donated some money. It does not matter that the gift was neither asked for nor even wanted. The person giving the gift will not even take it back because that would destroy the norm of reciprocation.

Has your family's Christmas card list grown longer each year through reciprocation? "Well, they sent us a card, so we better send them a card." Kunz and Woolcott (1976) sent Christmas cards to a large number of total strangers. More than 20% of the recipients sent back Christmas cards, despite the fact that the recipients did not know the original sender. Cards that appeared to come from high status senders (Dr. and Mrs.) were reciprocated at even higher levels.

Regan (1971) had two participants rate a number of paintings in an "art appreciation" study. In one condition, one of the persons (actually a confederate of the experimenter) left during a break and returned with two sodas, one for himself and one for the actual participant. In the other condition, the confederate returned from the break with nothing. After the experiment, the confederate asked the participant to buy some raffle tickets, mentioning that he (the confederate) could win a prize if he sold the most tickets. As you might guess, participants who received the soda bought almost twice as many tickets as those who received nothing. The reciprocity norm was more predictive of ticket buying than how much the participant liked the confederate.

Scarcity

Some of the things that collectors value the most are flawed items—misstruck coins, misprinted stamps, a baseball card with the player in the wrong uniform. These are items that normally might be regarded as trash, but become valuable and collectable because of their scarcity.

Sneaky influence occurs when we are presented with the *illusion* of scarcity. Look through a newspaper or magazine, or take a walk through a shopping area. How many "limited time offers" or "last chance, buy now" or "going out of business" advertisements do you see? All of these approaches are designed to make us "act now, before it's too late." If we don't hurry up and buy it, we'll never have another chance! For example, in the late 1990s, Disney advertised its *Pinocchio* video with the phrase "On video for the last time this century!" Reactance theory predicts that we will respond to this alleged scarcity and buy the product "while there's still time!"

Worchel, Lee, and Adewole (1975) demonstrated the effects of scarcity in a cookie-tasting experiment. Participants were given a jar that contained either two or ten chocolate-chip cookies and were asked to rate the quality of a cookie. Cookies from the short supply were rated as more attractive, more desirable to eat, and more expensive. Another group of participants was given a jar with ten cookies that was then replaced by a smaller jar with two cookies. These participants rated their cookies more favorably than those who had faced scarcity all along. Those who were told that the larger jar was taken to satisfy demand of other raters liked the cookies even more than participants who were told that the experimenter had simply miscounted. Scarce chocolate-chip cookies that other people like must really taste good!

Social Proof

You're going somewhere you've never been before, and you ask what other people will be wearing. We use the mode of social proof to determine what is correct by determining what other people think is correct. The method of social proof is a normal process that we use to gauge how to get along in society. When we find ourselves in unfamiliar situations, we often attend to the behavior of others and follow their lead. A sneaky form of social proof occurs when we simply follow along without analyzing or thinking about the situation. How often do you hear a product advertised as the best seller of its kind? The clear implication is, based on social proof, that we should buy that product.

Latané and Darley (1968) showed the effect of social proof in a stunning experiment. They had college men fill out a questionnaire in a room either alone or with two other men. Soon after the students began to work, the researchers pumped smoke into the room through a wall vent, wondering how quickly the students would report the smoke (there was a 6-minute time limit). In the solitary condition, 75% of the men responded by the end of the time limit, half within 2 minutes. In contrast, 62% of the groups continued working on their questionnaires for the entire 6 minutes, with only 1 person responding in less than 4 minutes. These results occurred despite the fact that the smoke was so thick at the end of 6 minutes that participants were coughing and could not see well. In an additional condition of the experiment, a subject participated (unknowingly) with 2 people who were confederates of the experimenters. These 2 people gave no reaction or response to the smoke regardless of the participant's behavior. In this condition, only

10% of the students reported the smoke. If 2 students appeared unconcerned about the smoke, that was apparently enough social proof for the participant. It appears that we may rely on social proof even when it could be deadly.

Critical Thinking Errors

Believing that we are immune from influence attempts violates Guideline 4 (separating facts from opinions). We cling to a belief in our own strength without considering the data. The research results in this chapter should help us face the facts. We are also guilty of not using Guideline 6 (making logical inferences). If we see that virtually everyone around us can be influenced, it is not particularly logical to think that we are somehow immune. If everyone else falls victim to influence attempts, it is logical to assume that we do also.

Thinking about Preconceptions

We are probably deluding ourselves if we have the preconception that we resist influence attempts and always make our own choices. Whether we like it or not, we are forced, by the evidence, to admit that our choices are often not completely our own. Our behaviors are influenced by other people.

A preconception about our invulnerability to influence is probably ill-advised for another reason: If we believe that we cannot be influenced, then we may let our critical thinking defenses down. Failing to analyze arguments and persuasion attempts will increase our susceptibility to persuasion.

Conclusion

This chapter emphasizes the power of the social situation—what David Myers called "the great lesson of social psychology" (1993, p. 214). As you look at Cialdini's principles of influence, note how each causes our behavior to be constrained by the situation.

Is it possible to resist the power of social influence? Can we make any decisions on our own without being influenced in some way? The evidence to answer that question affirmatively does exist, but it is clearly the minority position. It does seem possible, under some conditions, to resist the tug of social influence, but there are many variables and situations that can undermine this freedom. You must take the time to critically analyze a situation to determine whether influence is being used on you. Once you realize what is going on, you are in the position to short-circuit the persuasive attempt. Don't be disheartened, however, when you are bamboozled by one of these methods. Cialdini's book is filled with humorous examples of people influencing him. Hang in there—keep thinking and analyzing until you become an expert at resisting social influence.

Critical Thinking Exercises

1. Based on the information in this chapter, what steps can you take to become more resistant to social influence?
2. Think of a time when you fell victim to social influence. Describe the situation. What principle(s) helped weaken your resistance? Knowing what you know now, what would you do differently if the same situation occurred again?
3. Think about a car salesperson attempting to sell you a car. What techniques is this person likely to use? How can you circumvent those strategies?
4. Why do people give free samples of products at the grocery store? What social influence principle is being used? How is your behavior constrained in this situation?
5. Suppose you saw a car advertised by an individual for $1250. You desperately want the car but have only $1000 to spend. How would you attempt to influence this individual to lower the price to $1000 so you can buy the car? (Do not do anything illegal.)

References

Bickman, L. (1974). The social power of a uniform. *Journal of Applied Social Psychology, 4,* 47–61.

Cialdini, R. B. (2001). *Influence: Science and practice* (4th ed.). Boston: Allyn & Bacon.

Crandall, C. S. (1988). Social contagion of binge eating. *Journal of Personality and Social Psychology, 55,* 588–598.

Freedman, J. L., & Fraser, S. C. (1966). Compliance without pressure: The foot-in-the-door technique. *Journal of Personality and Social Psychology, 4,* 195–202.

Hofling, C. K., Brotzman, E., Dalrymple, S., Graves, N., & Pierce, C. M. (1966). An experimental study in nurse-physician relationships. *Journal of Nervous and Mental Disease, 143,* 171–180.

Janis, I. L., Kaye, D., & Kirschner, P. (1965). Facilitating effects of "eating-while-reading" on responsiveness to persuasive communications. *Journal of Personality and Social Psychology, 1,* 181–186.

Kunz, P. R., & Woolcott, M. (1976). Season's greetings: From my status to yours. *Social Science Research, 5,* 269–278.

Latané, B., & Darley, J. M. (1968). Group inhibition of bystander intervention in emergencies. *Journal of Personality and Social Psychology, 10,* 215–221.

Myers, D. G. (1993). *Social psychology* (4th ed.). New York: McGraw-Hill.

Myers, D. G. (1999). *Social psychology* (6th ed.). New York: McGraw-Hill.

Regan, D. T. (1971). Effects of a favor and liking on compliance. *Journal of Experimental Social Psychology, 7,* 627–639.

Worchel, S., Lee, J., & Adewole, A. (1975). Effects of supply and demand on ratings of object value. *Journal of Personality and Social Psychology, 32,* 906–914.

Looking toward the Future

Most books end with a conclusion or epilogue, and this book is no different—except for its title. I wanted to avoid using any title that conveys a sense of finality. Although you have now finished reading this book, I hope that you are *not* through using it! As I pointed out in the preface, there are many reasons why you need to think critically. Despite the fact this book has centered on critical thinking in the context of your psychology course, I believe that you can apply the skills you have learned here in a broader context.

It is in that broader context that it is essential for you to use your thinking skills. If you are like most students taking an introductory psychology class, you will not go on to graduate school in psychology or even major in psychology. You will, however, be faced with situations that demand critical thinking throughout the rest of your life, despite your choice of major or career. Life is only becoming more complex as time goes on. Rarely can we boil issues down to black-and-white choices. Thus, my advice is to continue to think about and challenge your preconceptions during the rest of your college career and throughout your life.

The good news about using your critical thinking skills is that such exercise appears to provide continuing benefits. Halpern (1996) summarized a variety of experimental evidence that indicates it is possible to improve critical thinking through various types of educational experiences. Presumably, that is why your instructor chose to use this text. More importantly, Halpern noted that evidence indicates that this critical thinking ability is transferable—that is, people who learn critical thinking skills can use them in different situations and for different types of knowledge than the original learning. However, as Halpern cautioned, "Critical thinking does not automatically result as a by-product of standard instruction in a content area" (p. 10). Therefore, it will be up to you to apply the thinking approaches and guidelines from this book in your other classes and life experiences in the future. Good luck in these ventures; I hope you have benefited (and will continue to benefit) from this approach to thinking.

Reference

Halpern, D. F. (1996). *Thought & knowledge: An introduction to critical thinking* (3rd ed.). Mahwah, NJ: Erlbaum.

Index

TO THE OWNER OF THIS BOOK:

I hope that you have found *Challenging Your Preconceptions: Thinking Critically about Psychology,* 2nd Edition, useful. So that this book can be improved in a future edition, would you take the time to complete this sheet and return it? Thank you.

School and address: _____

_____

Department: _____

Instructor's name: _____

1. What I like most about this book is: _____

_____

_____

2. What I like least about this book is: _____

_____

_____

3. My general reaction to this book is: _____

_____

_____

4. The name of the course in which I used this book is: _____

_____

5. Were all of the chapters of the book assigned for you to read?_____

   If not, which ones weren't? _____

6. In the space below, or on a separate sheet of paper, please write specific suggestions for improving this book and anything else you'd care to share about your experience in using this book.

_____

_____

_____

_____

OPTIONAL:

Your name: _____ Date: _____

May we quote you, either in promotion for *Challenging Your Preconceptions: Thinking Critically about Psychology,* 2nd Edition, or in future publishing ventures?

Yes: _____ No: _____

Sincerely yours,

Randolph A. Smith

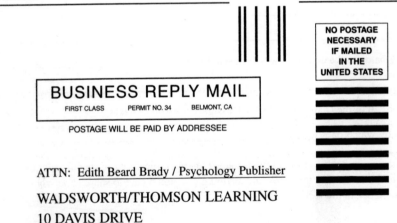